Dear Barb,

I hope you enjoy These stories. Dorel knows the author.

With love,

Lois 2/18/15

Bible Bits

Donna M. Evans

Ashway Press
Birmingham, Alabama

ASHWAY PRESS
BIRMINGHAM, ALABAMA

FIRST EDITION
Copyright 2012 Ashway Press, LLC

To order books or for information please contact our website:
www.ashwaypress.com

Book design by Kendra Peine Weeks
Cover photo of cup of coffee and wheat copyright by Istockphotos
Assitant Editing by Benjamin Weeks
Photos courtesy of Jennifer Hagler Photography, B'ham,Al. www.jenniferhaglerphoto.com
To contact the author: Donnamevans.com

Ashway Press, LLC.
Birmingham, Al. 35242
First Printing, June 2012

Printed in the United Sates of America
ISBN: 978-0-9754575-2-8

DEDICATION

(left to right) Coach Bruce Evans, Coach Sammy Dunn, Coach Peter Braasch

To Coach Sammy Dunn whose life inspired
many and whose death birthed Bible Bits.

James Bruce Evans, Jr. "Brucie"

ACKNOWLEDGEMENTS

No author writes a book alone and Bible Bits was written with lives before it was written with words. Many thanks to the following:

...to Linda and Sammy Dunn for opening their hearts and lives during a courageous 19 month battle with cancer.

... to a generous, supportive, and loving Vestavia Hills community for embracing the original Coach Dunn email updates and asking me to continue them after Coach Dunn's death.

...to every Bible Bits reader who read an email and encouraged me to keep writing. It still amazes me what God chooses to use.

...to the Wednesday night women's Bible study group whose prayer for me this year has been "focus and finish." By God's grace, those prayers have been answered.

...to Jennifer Hagler whose heart for special needs kids is matched only by her photography skill and craftsmanship.

...to Mama and Daddy who valued an education and sacrificed so greatly so that I could have one.

... to Meredith, Robert, and Daniel for your sacrificial love, tenderness, and service as siblings to a special needs brother.

...to Clay and Julia Hamblen for completing our family.

...to James Bruce who lives so close to God and constantly teaches me what God's grace and child-like faith are really all about.

...to Bruce for your faithfulness, wisdom, and steady hand in leading us and loving us well, especially me.

FOREWORD

In March, 2003 my husband's best friend and co-worker, Coach Sammy Dunn, was diagnosed with terminal stomach and liver cancer. Coach Dunn, a very successful and beloved high school baseball coach, was given just six-weeks to live.

At the time of Sammy's diagnosis, my youngest son, Daniel, was playing on the high school freshman baseball team. I started receiving daily telephone calls from parents wanting to know the latest information on Coach Dunn's condition. Because my husband, Bruce, was the junior varsity baseball coach, our home served as the central command post for disseminating information about Sammy's illness. This was before Caringbridge website days, and my phone rang constantly with people seeking updates on Coach Dunn's health crisis; I was quickly overwhelmed. Finally, frustrated with spending so much time on the phone, I passed around an email sign-up sheet at one of the freshman ballgames.

My goal was simple. Once a day I would send a global email update on Coach Dunn's condition. This way everybody could be "in the loop," and I could care for my own family's needs with the least amount of disruption. That was the plan...little did we know.

The list began with 15 freshman parent names. It soon morphed into more than double the original list as the varsity team's parents added their names. Word got out quickly to our loving and generous community, and more names were sent to me to be included on the email. When Coach Dunn's former students heard of his terrible illness, they wanted their names added. The only adjective that adequately describes the list's massive growth is "super natural." Thanks to the growing pool of resources, the Dunn's immediate needs were met.

Six-weeks passed quickly, and Coach Dunn was still very much alive. In fact, he was actually improving. The list was used to keep meals rotating to the Dunn home, and to meet some of their pressing needs. Meanwhile, the ever-growing list took on a life of its own.

Sammy's life focus shifted from baseball to telling others about Jesus. We were all praying for a divine deliverance for Sammy, but realized that it was more important to follow Sammy's lead in sharing the Gospel. Toward that end, I started putting a short Bible verse at the beginning of each Coach Dunn update. Knowing that God says that His Word will not return void without accomplishing that for which He sent it, I prayed and asked God to use His Word, Sammy's illness, and my email updates to bring Him glory.

Nineteen months later when Coach Dunn died in October 2004, the emails were going from California to Canada and everywhere in between. Something positive grew out of desperate need and extreme sorrow.

At Sammy's funeral, someone asked me if the emails, which had now evolved into more of a devotional, would continue. I quickly responded that Sammy was gone now, and there was really no reason to continue the emails. Someone else overheard our conversation, and immediately encouraged me to continue what God had started.

The next day I sent out the email devotional under the new title of *Bible Bits*. Surprisingly, the list continues to grow today. *Bible Bits* has literally become a journal for whatever God is teaching me in my everyday life as a working wife and mother. My husband, Bruce, and I have four adult children: Meredith, Robert, James Bruce (JB or Brucie), and Daniel. I have a B.S. degree in Pharmacy and work part-time at a local hospital.

James Bruce is often the instrument that God uses in my life to teach me more about Himself. James Bruce is a multi-challenged, disabled adult with autism, mild mental retardation, and seizure disorder. Although he weighs 165 pounds, he functions on a three or four-year-old level. James Bruce cannot read or write and must have constant supervision. He loves music and sees much of life from a child's perspective. He lives at home with us, and daily attends LINCPOINT, United Cerebral Palsy's (UCP) sheltered workshop for adults with disabilities.

Bible Bits continues to be a daily devotional. My initial goal was to keep the scripture reading to a "bite-size" piece so that readers would actually "read and feed" on God's Word. My life stories may inspire and encourage others, but only God's Word can truly change lives.

May God use both His Word and my family's stories to feed, encourage, and equip you to know, love, and serve Him. Our family purpose is to know God and make Him known to others. Toward this end, we offer our story for His glory.

From Him grace, to Him glory!
Donna Evans

FEAR

"Do not worry..." Matthew 6:25 (NIV)

✝

As James Bruce and I pulled out onto Highway 31 heading to work, the radio announcer said, "Here's your quote of the day from Corrie ten Boom: 'Worry does not empty tomorrow of its sorrow; it empties today of its strength.'"

Corrie ten Boom was a survivor of the German concentration camps. She and her family had hidden hundreds of Jews in Holland until they themselves were arrested. Her sister Betsie died at the hands of the Germans. Corrie survived and spent the rest of her life telling people about Jesus. Her life story is told in the inspirational movie *The Hiding Place*.[1]

I made a mental note of the quote and thought to myself, "I'll file that away for future reference. I'm not worrying about anything today except work." This was my morning's focus until Bruce called at 12:15. Our disabled son, James Bruce, was in trouble for hitting a fellow client. He was being suspended for three days, but they would count today as one of the days if I would come and get him right away. With that phone call, my afternoon turned upside down. My heart and head were racing with "what ifs."

"What if he gets totally kicked out of the UCP program?"
"What if Bruce has to go ahead and retire so he can keep him during the day?"
"What if I can't find 'child care' for the next two days?"
"What if I can't get all of my work done by a fast approaching deadline?"
"What if...what if...what if?"

The list continued as I sped down the freeway. All of a sudden, Corrie ten Boom's quote penetrated my mind, but this time, with some force, encouragement, and comfort:

"Worry does not empty tomorrow of its sorrow; it empties today of its strength."

I started praying God would help me respond with grace and not react in anger. Somehow, it helped remembering that while James Bruce's bad behavior caught me by surprise, it didn't catch God off guard. By the time I picked him up, my heart wasn't beating quite as fast and I really was calmer.

The staff was very gracious, apologetic even, as they described what led to the hitting incident. I thanked them, got James Bruce, and we headed home for the rest of the afternoon. I was still angry with him about his behavior. We got home and I sent him to his room for time-out. I was working my emotions back to a frantic state as I pondered what to do next. In the "discipline your emotions and do your next thing" mode, I grabbed a laundry basket and filled it with dirty clothes to take to the basement for washing. As I started down the steps, I saw the vase of white lilies in my foyer. When I got closer, their sweet perfume almost overwhelmed me. Suddenly Jesus' words against worry came to my mind and heart:

"Why do you worry about clothes? See how the lilies of the field grow. They do not labor or spin. Yet I tell you that not even Solomon in all his splendor was dressed like one of these. If that is how God clothes the grass of the field, which is here today and tomorrow is thrown into the fire, will he not much more clothe you, O you of little faith? So do not worry, saying what shall we eat? Or what shall we drink? Or what shall we wear?...your Father knows your need." Matthew 6:28-32 (NIV)

FEAR

"Do not fear, for I am with you;
Do not be dismayed for I am your God."
Isaiah 41:10 (NIV)

James Bruce had just gotten his shower and I was helping him get dressed. He was still damp, shivering like a wet dog, and his teeth were chattering frantically. I was trying to help him get his shirt on when he suddenly said, "Mama! Mama!"

Still trying to get his arms through the shirt, absently I responded, "What?"

"God told me what to say," James Bruce said.

I laughed as I finally got his arms through the shirt holes and asked him, "What did God tell you to say?"

Without a moment's hesitation, James Bruce replied, "Do not be afraid!"

"What did you just say?" I asked incredulously.

Firmly, he responded, "Do not be afraid!" With that exchange, my morning came to a stand still—a holy ground, burning-bush, take off your sandals, true "God speaks" moment. James Bruce had no way of knowing that just moments before, during my quiet time, I'd been in my Isaiah study. After plodding through the first 39 chapters of Isaiah's word to the Israelites concerning God's judgment, I'd finally made it to my study of chapters 40-66, often called "the book of consolation," and one of my favorite scripture passages.

There was no mistaking it—God's word for me today was "Do not be afraid." I now offer this same directive to you, not because it's my word, but because it's His. "Do not be afraid!" Of what?

Seizures	Job loss
Car wrecks	Catastrophic illness
Shaky economies	Singleness
Suffering	Retirement
Rebellious children	Old age

You can fill in the blank with your own fears. Beth Moore in one of her Bible studies once said, "To the person who fears God, there's no reason to fear anything or anyone else."

Franklin Roosevelt famously said, "The only thing we have to fear is fear itself." We can choose faith or we can choose fear, but we can't choose *both* at the same time. God's Word for all of us today is clear, commanding, challenging, and comforting:

"So do not fear for I am with you." Isaiah 41:10 (NIV)

FEAR

"I will be with you."
Genesis 31:3 (NIV)

God's promise to Jacob was one that Jacob relied on throughout his 147-year-life. God was with him as he ran away from Esau, lived in a foreign country, returned to Canaan with his family, and lived his last years under Joseph's care in Egypt. As he was dying his final words to his 12 sons were, "I am about to die, but God will be with you." (Gen 48:21 NIV). His confidence in God's promise to be with them surely provided comfort and consolation to his sons in the days and years ahead.

Jacob's words also provided a foundation for Moses' own words to the nation of Israel, as he, too, was about to die over 400 years later. "The Lord himself goes before you and will be with you; he will never leave you or forsake you. Do not be afraid; do not be discouraged." (Deut. 31:8 NIV)

As believers, whatever circumstances, we may find ourselves in, God's word is still true. "I will be with you." He, who has been with me in the past, is with me today and WILL be with me in the future. In fact, one of the names for Jesus is "Immanuel"—or God with us (Matt 1:23). God's promise and His presence should make a difference in the way I live. The choice is ours to make: faith or fear.

Jacob's example was an encouragement to me as our youngest son, Daniel, prepared to leave for college. My job as a parent is to keep pointing him to God (and away from me), reminding him that God will be with him too. As I do, I remind myself once again, that God will be with me, even as we faced a "semi-empty nest." With Brucie, we will probably never have a real empty nest, but life without Daniel is definitely different. Today, whatever you're facing, remember, "God is with me."

FEAR

"So do not fear, for I am with you; do not be dismayed, for I am your God.
I will strengthen you and help you. I will uphold you with
My righteous right hand." Isaiah 41:10 (NIV)

There are approximately 150 verses in the Bible where God says, "Do not fear." If God puts that much emphasis on our emotions, there must be a good reason. Perhaps it's because fear (or panic) is the first thing most of us do. It's the way we respond to our circumstances. The first recorded incident of fear is in the Garden after the fall of man. Adam's response to God is, "I was afraid,... so I hid." (Gen 3:10 NIV) Fear can do that to us—it can make us run, hide, panic, make poor choices, or paralyze us. Maybe this is why God tells us repeatedly, "do not fear." It can make us run *from* Him rather than *to* Him.

No matter what our circumstances are—death of a loved one, a serious illness, a handicapped child, a wayward kid, financial loss, or a deadly tsunami—God's promise is that He is with us. He is committed to hold our hand as we go through water (like the Red Sea) or through the river (like the Jordan River) or through the fire of affliction (like Daniel).

Elisabeth Elliot has wisely said, "Discipline your emotions and do the next thing." It is indeed a discipline, especially for women, to reel in our feelings, but God wants them and us under His control.

Today, whatever your circumstance, remember these words during your day:

> "In times of great difficulty and great
> expectation, it is our wisdom to keep our spirits
> calm, quiet and sedate; for then we are in the
> best frame both to do our own work and to
> consider the work of God." -Matthew Henry

FEAR

"The Lord is my shepherd, I shall not want."
Psalm 23:1 (NAS)

The word "want" means to fail to have, be without, or lack. The shepherd's job is to feed, guide, provide, protect, and, when necessary, to carry.

After my father's death, I knew provision beyond measure while My Shepherd carried *me* in His arms. Just as Barnabas saw the evidence of His grace (Act 11:23), so have I. Just to share a few:

1. A couple of days after Daddy's funeral, I had a desire for chicken salad, but didn't have the energy to make it or go get it. At 10:45 a.m. on a day I usually work, a friend showed up with two chicken salad take-out plates and said, "I thought you might like lunch."

2. I love spinach salad, but won't make it because the boys don't eat it. Three days in a row, someone from church brought spinach salad as part of our dinner. None of them knew what the other was bringing.

3. I love pound cake. My Daddy's mama always had pound cake on a glass cake plate in her farm kitchen. It was Daddy's favorite and mine too. Last Sunday, I thought about making one, but dismissed the idea in favor of a nap. When I got up from the nap, there was a plate of sliced pound cake on the kitchen table. Attached was a sympathy card, but the comfort came from knowing that God knows about my wants as well as my needs.

4. On the day of Daddy's funeral, we lost an important baseball game against a rival school. You'd think that the victor's players would get the big picture in the Saturday morning paper. Imagine my surprise, when my son Daniel, who only starts half of the time, got a huge color picture in a game that we lost.

God is not a genie that we can summon to give us our wishes, but He is a personal God who delights in being involved in the *details* of our lives.

Look for God to be at work in your life today. Join Him in His work, and don't forget to thank Him for the evidence of His grace.

"What we need to know, of course, is not just that God exists, not just that beyond the steely brightness of the stars there is a cosmic intelligence...but that there is a God right here in the thick of our day-by-day lives who may not be writing messages about Himself in the stars, but in one way or another, is trying to get messages through our blindness."[2] –Frederick Buechner

FEAR

"We do not know what to do, but our eyes are on you."
2 Chronicles 20:12 (NIV)

Three vast armies were coming to make war on King Jehoshaphat. The Bible says he was, "alarmed, but resolved to inquire of the Lord." (2 Chr. 20:3 NIV) He gathered his people, fasted and prayed, and acknowledged that he did not know what to do. Then they waited.

God answered in a mighty way. He commanded the Israelites to go out and face their enemies, and to stand and see His deliverance. As they obeyed, the opposing armies destroyed each other—all without one Jewish soldier lifting a weapon. God did exceedingly and abundantly beyond all they could think or imagine. It was an opportunity for His people to know God better.

How many times do I face situations, scared and not knowing what to do but looking, like Peter, at my circumstances and not my God? God wants his people to focus our eyes on Him and not on our circumstances.

God gave the King what he asked for—instructions on what to do next. Then He gave His people the deliverance that they had *not* asked for. We should expect no less. The key is asking Him for what we need and obeying what He tells us to do.

FEAR

"Afraid, yet filled with joy."
Matthew 28:8 (NIV)

We celebrated Easter last Sunday. My "sacred echo" throughout the day was the word "joy." That theme began with my early morning quiet time as I read Matthew's account of Jesus' death, burial and resurrection. As I read the passage, my focus was drawn to the women who followed Jesus. Matthew's account says there were "many women" who had followed Jesus from Galilee to "care for his needs." (Matthew 27:55) While the disciples fled in fear, the women watched Jesus' crucifixion from a distance. After Jesus' death on the cross, as evening approached, Mary Magdalene and another Mary watched Joseph of Arimathea carefully place Jesus' body in a new tomb. (Matt.27:57-61) Somehow, the women went home, prepared spices and perfumes, and "rested" on the Sabbath in "obedience to the commandment." (Luke 23:56) As soon as the Sabbath was over, the women returned to the tomb to finish anointing Jesus' body with the spices and perfumes. Just as they had done in life, they were now caring for His needs in death.

Imagine their surprise to find the tomb empty. Imagine their shock, when not just confronted by an angel, but also gently reprimanded. "Why do you seek the living among the dead?" (Luke 24:5 NIV) Then the reality of the resurrection set in and they hurried off in quick obedience to the angel's command, "Then go quickly and tell his disciples: 'He has risen from the dead and is going ahead of you into Galilee.'" (Matt 28:7 NIV)

There was fear, certainly, *yet* they were filled with joy. The joy of the reality of the resurrection, the joy of discovery and hope, the joy of obedience and blessing, and the joy of being entrusted with the good news of the gospel—He IS risen!

What's true for the women at the resurrection is still true for us today. God still calls us out of our comfort zones and entrusts us with the Good News of the gospel. Often we're afraid. Perhaps it's the "fear of the sneer." Maybe we don't feel like evangelism is our "spiritual gift." Often we feel inadequate or unworthy for the task. Whatever the reason, our fear paralyzes us and we miss the joy of obedience; the joy of blessing; the joy of discovery and having a part in God's work. Oh, that we would be like the women of the resurrection morning who were afraid, but not controlled by their fear. Their love for Jesus overcame their fear of man and the result was the JOY of obedience and blessing.

Wherever you are today, acknowledge your fear, but don't be controlled by it. Choose courage and combine it with quick obedience to whatever task God has assigned you. Then be filled with joy.

"Courage is not the absence of fear, but the conquest of it."
–John Croyle

He is risen; He is risen indeed!

REST

*"In repentance and rest is your salvation, in quietness
and trust is your strength." Isaiah 30:15 (NIV)*

After James Bruce had a massive seizure, I had some time to reflect and try to put the day's events in proper perspective. In doing so, the overwhelming take-away from the scary episode is that God meets us where we are.

That Sunday began with an all women's Sunday school class at the church. The morning speaker spoke on a range of topics, but she used Isaiah 30 as one of her main themes. I remember thinking, *rest is a good topic and I could use some more of it in my life.* This thought from an admittedly Type-A driven woman.

While in the women's class, I glanced through a brochure for an upcoming women's retreat. The retreat's theme was "choosing rest" and the theme verse was Isaiah 30:15 'in repentance and rest is your salvation.'

I didn't think a whole lot about the two "coincidences" until early Monday morning. It was 2 a.m. and I was in the emergency room with James Bruce. My body ached—a combination of fatigue, stress, and arthritis—and my mind and heart churned as I processed the last seven to eight hours' events. I kept reliving the whole sequence of the seizures' episode—at church, in the ambulance, in the ER hallway as we arrived, in the triage room, and now, in an ICU room. My body desperately wanted sleep, but my mind refused to allow it. I remember praying, "God, I need some sleep." Finally, I reached for my Bible and the women's retreat brochure fluttered to the floor. What I saw was, "Choosing rest."

Suddenly it hit me. When I couldn't choose sleep, I could still choose rest. God was with me in the emergency room. I wasn't alone. People were praying. James Bruce's outcome wasn't just up to me and my diligence or vigilance. I could press hard into God and *choose* rest. The words, "Be still and know that I AM God," (Psalm 46:10 NIV) came to my mind and was claimed by my heart. My tensed body could finally relax.

"Choosing rest" was my "sacred echo" for the following weeks. For the Christian, rest is not just a good gift from God, but it's also a choice. We can choose to "churn and burn" with anxiety, worry and stress or we can choose to rest in God's love, care, and strength. We can exchange our strength for His, but He leaves the choice to us.

Wherever you are today, in your office, home, carpool, school, or doctor's office, make a conscious choice to choose His rest. Rest in the knowledge that God knows where you are and that He means for you to be there. Find rest in His strength, love, care, and provision. God never promises to exempt us from our trials. He promises to go with us *through* them and to somehow use our adversity for our good and His glory.

Wherever you are today, choose His rest!

REST

"Come with me by yourselves to a quiet place
and get some rest." Mark 6:31 (NIV)

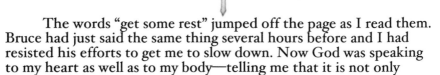

The words "get some rest" jumped off the page as I read them. Bruce had just said the same thing several hours before and I had resisted his efforts to get me to slow down. Now God was speaking to my heart as well as to my body—telling me that it is not only okay—but also necessary to get some rest.

Jesus' words to the disciples are still true for us today. It is a personal invitation to come away with Jesus. The only requirements are a willingness and obedience to go with him, a quiet place, and a desire to get some rest.

Richard Foster writes in his wonderful book *Celebration of Discipline*, "In contemporary society our Adversary majors in three things: noise, hurry, and crowds. If he can keep us engaged in 'muchness' and 'manyness,' he will rest satisfied."[3]

If we are willing to go with Jesus—away from the noise, the crowds, and the hurry—to spend time listening rather than talking, to *be* instead of *do*—He will give us the gift of His rest so that we are refreshed and equipped to meet the needs of each day.

"The Lord gave them rest on every side." Joshua 21:44 (NIV)

REST

"God has surely listened and heard my voice in prayer."
Psalm 66:19 (NIV)

All of the great Biblical characters were pray-ers that were driven by their needs to their knees. With Jehoshaphat, there was the fear of destruction by war; with Hannah, it was her infertility; with Moses, it was the loss of God's presence as they journeyed to the Promised Land. In each case, the following principles were evident:

1. Their situation was hopeless without God's intervention.
2. They knew that nothing is impossible with God.
3. They brought the request to God.
4. They knew that God heard them.
5. There was a period of waiting on God.
6. They expected God to act.
7. They praised Him for His answer.
8. They experienced the joy of obedience and the rewards of victory.
9. They ultimately knew God better after the adversity, prayer, and answer.
10. God got the glory.

God hasn't changed. The same principles that have guided God's people in the past are still relevant for us today. God still waits to act for those who are willing to ask Him and wait on Him. (Isaiah 64:4)

What about you? What impossible situation do you need to bring to Him today? He still listens and hears our voices in prayer, but He still expects us to ask, not for information, but rather transformation.

Keep asking!

PROVISION

*"Now to Him who is able to do far more abundantly
beyond all that we ask or think."*
Ephesians 3:20 (NAS)

When Daniel was two-weeks-old, it was time to write our monthly tithe check. I told Bruce that with two children in diapers, we could tithe, but we'd have to make a choice between eating and diapering our babies.

His response was typical Bruce, "Write the check."

There was no use arguing with him, so I wrote the tithe check. As I did, I prayed, "Lord, we're in trouble. We can eat or we can buy diapers, but we can't do *both*. Bruce says you know exactly where we are, so here we are." In my mind, I had God boxed in: He would potty-train four-year-old James Bruce and this was truly my preference; God would send some extra money (that answer works for me every time); or we'd go under, and honestly, that's what I expected to happen.

The next day Bruce came home from school. I was nursing two-week-old Daniel. As Bruce came through the front door, he called out, "Come see what I've got in the driveway." I protested that I was nursing the baby and he responded, "Bring the baby and come see my surprise."

I grumbled the whole way out until I saw what was in our driveway. Bruce had an old 1978 long-bed, blue, Chevrolet pickup truck. The whole back of the truck was full of DIAPERS! Every brand, every size—over 1500 diapers were in the back of his truck. Enough diapers so that we didn't buy a single diaper for four months.

"Where did these come from?" I asked incredulously.

"The faculty," he said. "They surprised me this afternoon with a shower. They said every Dad deserves to be 'Pampered!'"

It was another one of those "holy ground" moments—the kind where God does indeed meet me where I am in my ordinary life and turns it into something extraordinary—not because of who I am, but because of who He is. In God's hands, something as ordinary as a baby's diaper becomes a family's memorial stone that points us to God for who He is and what He's done. Whenever things get tight—financially, emotionally, spiritually, or physically—the diaper story reminds me that God IS faithful; that He's able to meet our needs in ways that I can't even begin to imagine, and that He is God—He does it His way, not my way. In the end, God's ways are ALWAYS better than our own.

PROVISION

"The Lord did what he had promised."
Genesis 21:1 (NIV)

My oldest son, Robert, was involved in an automobile accident that demolished his car. Although he was physically unharmed, trying to find a replacement car for Robert and settling with the insurance company proved to be a daunting task. All of us—except James Bruce—were keeping our eyes and ears open trying to find the *right* car at the right price. We became very discouraged as we prayed and searched for a car to fit our tight budget.

During this aggravating process, I recalled how a then seven-year-old Robert had earnestly prayed for a blue van. As a family who needed a second vehicle, we prayed for any decent car, but Robert insisted it *had* to be a blue van. When we finally bought a good used car, sight unseen, from an uncle in Georgia (his elderly aunt had moved to a nursing home), Robert wasn't surprised when his daddy pulled up in a blue van. I was stunned, of course, but I have never forgotten the impression the incident left on our family. Could it happen twice?

I was pondering this issue when our phone rang. A baseball dad hesitantly asked if we had found a car for Robert. I said "No" and he told me about the car that he was selling. He had just gotten a company car, so he no longer needed his. The price was right, and so was the car. Less than 24 hours later, Robert had his car. He also had a memorial stone in his life. A memorial stone is a visual reminder of God's faithfulness. It reminds us of a time when we faced an impossible situation, God called us to step out in faith, we obeyed, and God delivered in a way that brings glory to Himself. As Robert drives this car, I pray that he is reminded every day of God's faithfulness, grace and provision.

PROVISION

"You are the God who sees me."
Genesis 16:13

It's important to remember that God sees us not only as we are, but He also sees us *where* we are.

When Hagar uttered these words of faith, she was in the desert—pregnant and alone. God came to her and asked her two questions: "Where have you come from, and where are you going?" (Gen 16:8) God didn't ask her because He needed to know; out of love, He asked her because SHE needed to know the answer to both questions.

There are times in all our lives when we, like Hagar, must evaluate where we've been and where we're going. When we do that honestly before God, He will show us what to do just as He showed Hagar. The choice is then ours—to go our own way or God's way.

May we, like Hagar, respond in faith and obedience to our God who always sees us wherever we are.

PROVISION

"Your Father knows what you need."
Matt 6:8 (NIV)

This verse has carried me through the last two days. I knew when I left the house yesterday morning that my schedule was packed. I remembered when God told Solomon, "Ask whatever you want me to give to you." (1 Kings 3:5) Solomon knew exactly what he wanted from God—and he received the wisdom that he had requested. I realized I had many needs, but I still wasn't sure which need was the greatest. It was comforting to remember that as my Father, He already knew my need(s). He wasn't waiting on me to compile a list for Him, but to simply admit that I had many needs. I decided to ask for strength and grace.

Before the day ended, my Daddy's outpatient procedure landed him in the hospital's intensive care unit. In addition, my son, Daniel, was scheduled to play in two baseball games. I couldn't be in both places at the same time. Still there was *the* voice—"Your Father knows what you need." By the time I got home, two people had called from the church to let me know they were praying for our family. I didn't even know who could have possibly called our church, but I felt loved and cared for anyway—surrounded by people willing to babysit JB or fix a meal—carried along by His everlasting arms.

This morning, on my desk, was a CD that my oldest son, Robert, had created and simply labeled "Mom." I grabbed it up on my way out the door and put it in the CD player. Nicole Nordeman's song, *Gratitude,* was the first song. She sings about asking God for one thing and often getting another—and still being grateful. In one line, she says, "Oh the differences that often are between what we want and what we really need."[4]

I don't know what your need is today—perhaps it's healing, salvation for a loved one, restoration of a broken relationship, patience, financial, or maybe just enough time to do the things somebody requires of you—but God, our Father, knows where we are *and* our needs. He wants us to trust Him, take Him at His word, and be grateful for not only His answer, but also His provision.

PROVISION

"I myself will tend my sheep."
Ezekiel 34:15 (NIV)

"Go out each day and gather enough for that day."
Exodus 16:4 (NIV)

God promises us that He assumes personal responsibility for tending to or taking care of His sheep. Ezekiel 34 is a wonderful chapter that lists all of the things a good shepherd does: gathers, leads, feeds, protects, brings back the lost, strengthens the weak, binds up the injured, and provides safety and security for his flock.

As comforting as this passage is, the other side is that we have a personal responsibility as well. In Exodus 16, God supernaturally provided food in the wilderness for the Israelites. It was called manna—the bread from heaven. All the people had to do was to go out and gather it each day. If they waited too long, the sun would rise and melt away the manna leaving everyone hungry until the next day.

In the same way, God calls *us* to gather enough of His truth for today. His Word is still the Bread of Life and we are to feast on it daily. No one can do that for us. We have to open our Bibles and read.

There are devotional books, sermons, emails, and other tools that can challenge and encourage you—but only God can feed you from His Word. He wants to do this, but we must be willing to come and to gather on a daily basis.

"Open your mouth wide and I will fill it." Psalm 81:10 (NIV)

PROVISION

"God Himself will provide...The Lord will provide."
Gen 22:8, 14 (NIV)

Several needs, each involving my children, have pressed and distressed me over the last few days. I've prayed and nothing seems to be happening on any front. The needs vary—finding a replacement car for Robert, getting James Bruce's placement at UCP for the fall session, praying Meredith through year-end closeout (the equivalent to tax season for corporate CPAs), settling the AP physics teacher situation for Daniel—nothing earth shattering or life threatening, but collectively they add up to a heavy weight that I cannot fix. I pray and wait, fret and fume, and sometimes I even try to fix it myself before reverting to praying and waiting again.

The irony—as well as these verses—hit me yesterday morning in my quiet time. I was preparing to teach a study on the prayers of great pray-ers. One of the key elements Moses, David, Hannah, Elijah, Nehemiah, Daniel, and Paul had in common was that they often had a waiting period AFTER they had prayed. I'm learning in God's classroom that waiting and praying—the process—is something harder to practice than to study or teach.

The truth is that God Himself will provide for us just as He provided for Abraham's offering. He has promised to do so, and He cannot lie. It doesn't matter how hopeless the situation or how desperate our need. God is the great provider for His people. Whatever the need in your own life, He wants you to ask Him for it. Beth Moore says God always answers prayer—either to demonstrate His supremacy or His sufficiency. He doesn't always give us what we ask for, but He gives us what we need.

"On the mountain of the Lord, it will be provided."
Genesis 22:14 (NIV)

PROVISION

*"God wants all men to be saved and to come to a
knowledge of the truth." 1 Timothy 2:4 (NIV)*

Recently while vacationing in Gatlinburg, Tennessee, I
experienced firsthand culture shock. I'm not just talking different
skin colors and languages—I mean tattoos, navel rings, body
piercings, and mohawks. I was offended by a lot of the language that
I heard and repulsed by some of the actions that I witnessed. In
short, I wanted to retreat to my world at home—somewhat insulated,
isolated, and protected from the culture that shocked and offended
me.

One night, as Bruce and Daniel were playing a game of pool, I
was upstairs reading in my Bible. I had the door open to the deck
where Brucie sat rocking and singing in the darkness while looking at
the stars above. I can't remember most of what he sang, but when he
got to one song, I stopped and listened:

"Jesus loves the little children,
All the children of the world,
Red and yellow, black and white,
They are precious in his sight,
Jesus loves the little children of the world."

I have sung that song since I was a four-year-old in Sunday
school, but God used it that night to show me my judgmental,
critical, and condemning attitudes toward others. He reminded me
that He does indeed love all men and desires none to perish. While
He hates sin, He always loves the sinner. I should do no less.

One practical way I can do this is to pray rather than judge or
condemn. This, after all, is God's responsibility—not mine.

PROVISION

"You gave abundant showers, O God; you refreshed
your weary inheritance." Psalm 68:9 (NIV)

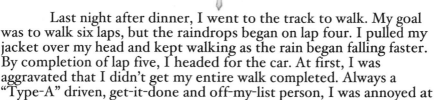

Last night after dinner, I went to the track to walk. My goal was to walk six laps, but the raindrops began on lap four. I pulled my jacket over my head and kept walking as the rain began falling faster. By completion of lap five, I headed for the car. At first, I was aggravated that I didn't get my entire walk completed. Always a "Type-A" driven, get-it-done and off-my-list person, I was annoyed at the first drops of rain. God quickly reminded me how we had prayed for rain throughout the summer, and how much it was needed, even if His timing didn't agree with mine. By the time I got home, it was pouring and I was truly thankful for the rain.

This morning my lawn and plants looked so much healthier and greener. They had been refreshed by the rain. In much the same way, our souls and hearts are refreshed by God's Word and Spirit, when we spend time with Him. The Apostle Peter declared that, "times of refreshing may come from the Lord." (Acts 3:19 NIV) and Ezekiel spoke of "showers of blessing" (Ezekiel 34:26). The Greek word for "refresh" literally means "relief, relaxation, and refreshment."

I don't know about you, but most days, I get weary from the demands of work, family, needs, errands, and schedule. I need to be refreshed and renewed. Sometimes it is hard to carve out the time to spend with God, but every time I do, I come away with a renewed spirit, abundant energy, a dose of courage, and grace to keep going. God promises us, "I will pour water on the thirsty land and streams on the dry ground; I will pour out my Spirit on your offspring and my blessing on your descendents." (Isaiah 44:3 NIV)

If you're dry and thirsty, weary, tired and ready for some relief and refreshment, spend a few minutes with God. May His presence and Spirit revive and renew you for the demands of your day.

"Those who hope in the Lord will renew their strength."
Isaiah 40:31 (NIV)

PROVISION

"Gather the pieces that nothing may be lost."
John 6:12 (NAS)

Jesus had just finished feeding 5,000 people with five loaves of bread and two small fish, yet He commanded the disciples to gather up the pieces. When they finished, 12 baskets were *full* of broken pieces. I've often wondered why Jesus told them to do this. Was it an exclamation point on the end of the miracle? Why did Jesus choose to use a small boy's lunch to start with? Why did the One who spoke the world into being not just speak to stones and turn them into bread?

Over the years as I've gone back to this passage repeatedly, I am once again reminded that God cares about the pieces of our lives. Just as He commanded the disciples to gather their pieces, so He commands us today. Whether it's the pieces from a failed marriage, a disappointing start to a football season, a rebellious or special needs child, a financial crisis, or the aftermath of a devastating hurricane— God cares about the leftover pieces. He tells us today, as he told the disciples then, "Gather up the pieces that nothing may be lost." The gathering and giving them to Him is our responsibility; what He does with the pieces is God's part. Once in His hands, He can use the pieces for our good and for His glory.

"Knowing what to do must be translated into doing what you know." -Bruce Wilkinson

32

LEGACY

"Choose you this day who you will serve;
but for me and my house, we will serve the Lord."
Joshua 24:15 (NIV)

My Uncle Bob died at the age of 78 after battling a cancerous brain tumor for 13 months. Somewhere during the time of chemotherapy and radiation, his grandson filmed a video of Uncle Bob telling various stories from his life. Mama and three of her other siblings, along with my sister and two cousins, flew to Texas for his funeral. Everyone came back telling stories: stories of their childhood, stories of Uncle Bob's life, and stories of their trip together.

Of all the stories that I heard, one in particular stands out in my mind and heart. My maternal grandparents were in their childbearing years during the Great Depression. Born in 1932, Uncle Bob was greatly influenced by the aftermath of the Depression. In his video, he recalled one Easter when my grandparents couldn't afford Easter baskets. Undaunted, Granddaddy dug holes out in the yard, filled them with straw from the barn, and Grandmother filled the makeshift "baskets" with dyed eggs from the chickens that lived in the barn. I've heard of *dirt poor*, but all of a sudden, the term came alive. It also helped explain why *things* were so important to my uncle. He worked hard, but he also liked buying a lot of nice things.

Six months prior to the funeral, someone from a local church asked me to come speak at their women's retreat. We covered a lot of Scripture and biblical principles in our sessions, but God's nudging to "tell the story" caused me to use more personal stories than I usually share. I hesitate to share too many Evans' stories because I never want people to glorify us, but God reminded me last week, that our stories are really His.

One of the women's favorites was of James Bruce singing (via video) Amazing Grace in a Sunday morning worship service and then looking at me declaring, "I was the star!" Bruce and I had been praying for six years that God would somehow use James Bruce for His glory. It seemed like an impossible prayer for the parents of a special needs child with autism and mental deficiencies. We'd also been praying that God would enable us to find one area in which James Bruce could excel. It turns out that music is his *thing* and he really loves hymns. Somehow, God connected the dots and allowed James Bruce to be featured in a Special Ones ministry highlight video that was played during both worship services, answer a broken Mama's prayer, and help a special needs child feel good about himself. The whole event was a "holy ground" moment for me, a memorial stone event for our family, and truly God's Amazing Grace, not just in song, but in real life time and space.

All of us have stories that need to be protected, preserved and passed on to coming generations. The best stories are real, raw, and redemptive. They're life lived—not life invented. They point future generations away from us and toward God.

What are you doing to preserve your life stories? Are you prepared to share them and store them, either in writing or per video? If not, ask God to meet you where you are and give you a story for His glory—one that reminds you and those who follow you, that God is God, that He is faithful, and He is able to do more than we can think or imagine.

LEGACY

"A good man leaves an inheritance for his children's children."
Proverbs 13:22 (NIV)

This verse came to mind one Friday night about midnight as I lay in the dark at our family lake house. Upstairs I could hear Daniel and seven baseball teammates laughing and talking. Some of them were playing foosball while others were playing music or video games. I kept thinking about my Dad and his wisdom in building the lake house.

Daddy looked at the lake house as an investment, not just in real estate, but in building family relationships. Daddy was a blue-collar railroad man who was also good at building things. He built the house himself and paid for it as he did so. We spent many hours together as a family doing whatever needed to be done to finish it. In the process, Daddy built our family as well as the lake house. Through the years, Daddy used the lake house as a gathering place for church groups, family reunions, and birthday parties. He gave each of us the gift of *place* when he opened his heart and home to whatever group needed the house. Now I am trying to follow his example.

About the time things settled down for the night upstairs, I heard some singing downstairs. It was James Bruce singing in the next bedroom. Bruce and I strained to hear the words as *El-Shaddai* led into *Our God is an Awesome God*, and then finally *Amazing Grace*. All in the dark and to an audience of One, Brucie sang himself to sleep. I was overwhelmed with God's goodness and my Dad's provision in giving my children and me both a physical and spiritual inheritance.

LEGACY

"What is to be the rule for this boy's life and work?"
Judges 13:12 (NIV)

✝

Manoah's prayer for Samson has certainly become one of my favorite prayers for my children, especially today as James Bruce "graduates"—well, actually ages-out is more appropriate—from high school. It is comforting to know that just as Manoah asked for God's guidance for his child, so can I. The God, who heard then, still hears now. Not just for James Bruce, but for any child entrusted to a parent, for any age, and any stage. God waits for us to ask on behalf of our children—for direction, guidance, and instruction. In doing so, I acknowledge my dependence on Him to do those things that I cannot while remaining teachable to do those things that I can— pray, train, and teach, plan, and prepare as much as possible.

In many ways, like other graduates, we are stepping into the unknown, moving from the safe and familiar, and taking the next step of faith. After a summer at the Exceptional Foundation, Brucie will attend LINCPOINT, a daily sheltered adult workshop at the United Cerebral Palsy Center.

LEGACY

"To me to live is Christ, to die is gain." Philippians 1:21 (NIV)

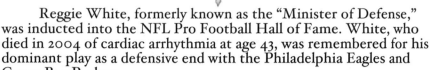

Reggie White, formerly known as the "Minister of Defense," was inducted into the NFL Pro Football Hall of Fame. White, who died in 2004 of cardiac arrhythmia at age 43, was remembered for his dominant play as a defensive end with the Philadelphia Eagles and Green Bay Packers.

"Reggie White was a gentle warrior who will be remembered as one of the greatest defensive players in NFL history," NFL Commissioner Paul Tagliabue said. "Equally as impressive as his achievements on the field was the positive impact he made off the field and the way he served as a positive influence on so many young people."[5]

How Reggie White lived, was with *passion* and *purpose*. He filled up a room, not by his size, but with his presence. If you were fortunate enough to have met him, you couldn't forget him. Bruce and I had the pleasure of meeting him in the early eighties at FCA camp in Black Mountain, N.C. when he was still playing at the University of Tennessee. Reggie was there to share his personal testimony and challenged hundreds of teenage athletes to consider a personal relationship with Jesus Christ. He had a huge smile, an infectious laugh, and an appeal that went beyond the football field. When he spoke, people listened.

Reggie White's life was one of excellence, both on and off the field. He knew Christ and wanted to make him known. That's why his wife could say with confidence, "live like Reggie lived." What about us? If we died today, could our family members, our neighbors, coworkers, and friends, say with confidence and conviction, "Live like he/she did." May we, like the Apostle Paul, and Reggie White live such a life of excellence, purpose, and passion that "And by faith he still speaks, even though he is dead." (Hebrews 11:4 NIV)

LEGACY

"Great is thy faithfulness."
Lamentations 3:23 (NIV)

The church I grew up in recently celebrated its 100th anniversary. Founded in 1907 with approximately 50 members, the church is now home to over 6,000 folks.

As part of the centennial celebration, the church hosted a reception for former members. There was a wonderful display of the church's history through ten decades. A beautiful quilt made in 1932 was included in the exhibit. The quilt had a lovely white background with dozens of names embroidered in blue. I was amazed at the detail, craftsmanship, preservation and the story associated with the quilt. Some enterprising women decided to charge a dime to have your name put on the quilt. The dime was then donated to the church building fund. Now keep in mind, this was the middle of the Great Depression. Not only was the quilt a true labor of love, it was a gift of sacrifice. Someone had lovingly preserved all that history. The names once written on the quilt are now written in the heavens forever.

A homemade wedding dress was featured in the 1940's display, along with World War II uniforms. The dress was elegant in its simplicity and I was captivated by the resourcefulness of the mama who crafted it. The wedding gown had been carefully preserved and handed down to the next generation of women. I marveled at the contrast between the simplicity of the 1940's gown and wedding dresses of today.

A time capsule from 1957 was opened so the contents could be displayed. There was a key to the city, some photographs, a Baptist hymnal, and some books. My favorite things in the time capsule were the notes from church members. Hundreds of cards with thoughts and prayers for 50 years in the future were alphabetically displayed on bulletin boards. My mama found hers. She had written that she hoped the church would continue to enjoy God's blessing and growth. I think God heard and answered that prayer.

It's really hard to imagine how much has changed since 1907. The church has changed physical locations at least four times. Businesses no longer advertise in the church bulletin as they did in the one displayed from 1927. Members no longer donate their proceeds from the sale of *real* cow's milk and homemade butter as they did in 1932, nor does the whole church turn out to find the cow if it gets lost. (That anecdote was featured in the centennial video). Pastors have come and gone and so have thousands of members. The one constant has been God Himself—He never changes.

"You shall love the Lord your God with all your heart and with all your soul and with all your mind...You shall love your neighbor as yourself." (Matthew 22:37, 39 ESV)

That's not just a great passion; it's a great purpose and prayer. To God be the glory.

LEGACY

*"God is our refuge and strength, an ever-present help in trouble.
Therefore we will not fear, though the earth give way and the
mountains fall into the heart of the sea, though its waters roar
and foam and the mountains quake with their surging."*
Psalm 46: 1-2 (NIV)

One of my favorite talks when I speak to young moms' groups is a series entitled, "CALM in the CHAOS." These tender moms with toddlers and preschoolers are often overwhelmed with the 24/7 demands of small children—the messes, the stresses, and the seemingly unending drain of time, money and emotions. The CALM principle is an acronym that stands for Christ Always Loves Me. Many times in our household when our own four children were younger and life was falling apart at the seams, I would count off on four fingers and literally chant, "Christ always loves me, Christ always love me." The circumstances might not change immediately, (as when each of my children took turns having chicken pox for the three weeks before Easter) but somehow my spirit would be calmer and more resilient.

Over the years, an acronym also developed for the CHAOS part of the seminar. God showed me the following characteristics were typically in play when there was chaos in my life.

Confusion
Harried or hurried
Attitude of Anger
Out of control
Shock or Self-Absorption

Recognizing the symptoms of chaos helped me to begin to pray more specifically and practice the CALM principle. It also led to opportunities to share some practical suggestions for effectively dealing with life's chaos.

LEGACY

"I thank Christ Jesus our Lord, who has given me strength,
that he considered me faithful, appointing me to His service."
1 Timothy 1:12 (NIV)

Friday morning found me at the coffee shop meeting my friend Beth. We've been friends since college. After college, we relocated to the same small town, and raised our babies together. We've married children, buried parents, and seen each other through moves and career changes. Beth lives in another city now so we don't get to see each other often. When we do, however, we just pick right back up where we left off the last time we were together.

As Beth sat down in the booth, she exclaimed to me, "I just want to FINISH WELL. I want to be faithful!" With that, she handed me two pairs of socks, and told me her husband, Bobby, sent Bruce and me each a pair of socks.

"What's this for?" I asked.

"It's our new FITS® sock line," she replied.

Together we chanted, "Faithful, Intentional, Teachable, Servant." We both laughed as I moved the FITS® socks off the table and we moved on to talk about other things. While we were talking, I saw the founding pastor of my church come into the restaurant. I could tell he was looking for someone as he sat down quietly and put his Bible on the table. I caught his eye and he smiled and briefly waved. In just a few minutes, a younger man arrived with his own Bible. For the next hour, the two of them sat there quietly, talking and reading from their Bibles amidst the hustle and bustle in the busy restaurant.

As Beth and I continued talking, it hit me. My pastor is a living, walking, true "FITS®": a Faithful, Intentional, and Teachable Servant. Not only had he founded and grown a mega-church, he had also preached to millions of people around the world. Now he had stepped away from the pulpit after 40 years of preaching, but he never stepped away from teaching, evangelism, or service. Here he was on a Friday morning, away from the spotlight or crowds, meeting one-on-one with a younger man, transferring truth intentionally and relationally from one generation to the next. By the end of this weekend, I would have seen him several times in different family and church venues. Each time his message was always the same—God is faithful and to God be the glory! The message was always delivered with grace and gratitude.

Last night I came home and tried on my new FITS® socks. They are undoubtedly the best socks I've ever worn. They actually FIT just as their name claims. Every time I wear the socks, I will think of my pastor and his legacy of a lifetime: Faithful, Intentional, Teachable, and a Servant.

What about you? Do you want to finish well, and are you a FITS®? To the one who does indeed finish well, Jesus says, "Well done, thou good and faithful servant... enter into the joy of thy Lord." (Matthew 25:21 KJV)

LEGACY

"Use whatever gift you have received to serve others."
1 Peter 4:10 (NIV)

Our brood enjoys trips to the family beach house for some much needed rest, fun, and family time. My high-strung nature normally doesn't allow me to nap during the day, but the salt tinged ocean air mandates a daily nap for all. Bruce's mom, Mimi, has four wonderful handcrafted quilts stored away in the beach house closets. Each day I'd choose a different one and find myself wondering about the quilt's history.

The quilts were made by Bruce's grandmother, Mee-Maw. I only knew her briefly because she died our second year in college. She was barely five-feet-tall, but she scared me to death anyway. Her culinary skills were legendary, but I was unaware of her sewing talents until I started inquiring about the quilts.

On my favorite quilt, I counted at least 31 different fabrics woven into the design. Purple seemed to be her favorite color for the backing and fabric strips, but there were all kinds of other colors and fabrics mixed in. Baby quilt scraps of pink, blue, green, and yellow merged with royal blue curtain material. Even her aprons weren't spared as she sacrificed their orange and gray calico patterns to the evolving quilt. Hand-sewn housedresses relinquished their brown and ivory gingham fabric scraps, while swatches from the striped men's pajama set contributed to the overall eclectic design of the one-of-a-kind quilt. My favorite fabric in the festive, colorful, hand-made quilt was the "Davy Crockett" material—complete with coonskin hat and rifle—a contribution from my husband's little toddler blanket. The overall quilt "pattern" was random, but the net effect was what Bruce's mother, Mimi, endearingly refers to as "Folk art."

I found myself lying on the beach and thinking often of the quilts and their maker. How many thousands of hand stitches were sewn into the quilts? How long did it take to complete one? Did she recognize their beauty and her extraordinary talent? Finally, did Mee-Maw ever dream that some half-century later, her children, grandkids, and great-grandchildren—three generations—would be using and enjoying them, wondering about her life and marveling at her skills?

Bruce's Aunt Jean came over one night and provided some background and insight into the quilts' origin and history. Mee-Maw was a Great Depression survivor who hated waste, choosing to use what she already had instead of buying new. She essentially recycled fabrics and garments before recycling became popular. Quilting was

Mee-Maw's recreational outlet as each Thursday morning she headed to her church to socialize with other devoted women quilters.

As I reflected on Mee-Maw's creativity and artistry, I finally concluded she had used her gifts wisely to help others. This led me to reflect upon my own gifts. Do I choose to use my special talents to help others? Where are "the quilts" in my own life—those things, which could bless future generations? At first, I was somewhat melancholy about the piercing questions, but God, ever faithful, led me to today's verse:

> "Each one should use whatever gift he has received to serve others, faithfully administering God's grace in its various forms. If anyone speaks, he should do it as one speaking the very words of God. If anyone serves, he should do it with the strength God provides, so that in all things God may be praised through Jesus Christ. To Him be the glory and the power forever and ever. Amen." 1 Peter 4:10-11 (NIV)

LEGACY

✝

Brucie and I ran to the grocery store to pick up a few items. I barely made it past the grocery carts before I saw a huge sign that read "Blackberries—regular $3.99, now 99 cents." One woman was already filling her cart with the beauties. I paused and remembered my Granny Muir's blackberry cobbler. Granny's pound cake was her signature dessert. We affectionately called it "Granny cake." Her next best dessert and hands down, "go to" recipe was her homemade blackberry cobbler. My siblings, cousins and I would pick blackberries at the farm down by Papa's spring. We'd bring them back to Granny and she'd make a blackberry cobbler. The pie was sweet, but not too sweet, and the crust was to die for! Whenever I see blackberries, I fondly remember my Granny lovingly creating these treats.

When the lady in front of me finally finished loading her buggy, I picked up two cartons and carefully looked at the blackberries. Honestly, the blackberries were the size of quarters—much larger than the ones I used to pick at the farm. They were big, plump, and juicy—not bruised or running. I stood there and realized that I'd been married for 35 years, and I had NEVER made a blackberry cobbler. I waivered as I tried to decide if I wanted to invest my money, time, and resources on a memory. My memories finally won out and I bought two containers, reasoning that if I failed or flopped, I'd only lost $2.

Once home I searched the Internet for a recipe. I settled on "Easy Blackberry Cobbler." I wasn't sure how the cobbler would taste, but it sure was easy to put together. A milk, flour, butter batter on the bottom with sugar-soaked blackberries sprinkled on the top, baked at 375 degrees for 45 minutes and voila—a blackberry cobbler! Even better was the fact that I put the pie on timed-bake so that it was hot and ready when we came in from the ballpark. I never expected it to taste like Granny's pie—and it didn't—but it was so good that I made three cobblers that week. With each one, I've thought about my Daddy and his mom. The cobblers have resurrected memories of people and incidents long forgotten. They also brought me comfort as I reflected on the anniversary of Daddy's death.

Holy Week is a time we remember the death, burial and resurrection of Jesus. It is a good time to trace Jesus' daily steps on that first Holy Week; from the crowd's "hosannahs" on Palm Sunday to the resurrection on the next Sunday. Jesus, my Savior, set His face like flint and moved intentionally toward the cross to take my place. Maundy Thursday is the day we remember Jesus' last Passover meal with His disciples. In an upper room, Jesus ate with His disciples and washed their feet. At that time, He took the Passover bread and said, "This is my body, which is given for you; do this in remembrance of Me." Later He took wine and said, "This cup is the new covenant in my blood; do this, whenever you drink it, in remembrance of me. For whenever you eat this bread and drink this cup, you proclaim the Lord's death until He comes." (1 Corinthians 11:24-26 NIV)

Much like the blackberry cobblers reminded me of my Granny and my Daddy, the Lord's Supper is designed to help us remember Jesus' atoning death on the cross. When we eat the communion bread, we're reminded that Jesus is indeed the Bread of Life. When we drink the communion wine, we're reminded of His first miracle at the wedding of Canaan. We're also reminded that Jesus said, "If any man thirsts, let him come to Me and drink." (John 7:37 KJV) The communion food is designed to help us remember why we celebrate Easter. The Lord's Supper is a tool to help us remember Jesus—his life, death, resurrection and coming again. The communion food triggers our memory and gives us comfort and encouragement.

This Sunday may find you gathered with loved ones, sharing an Easter meal, laughing and enjoying food and fellowship. Wherever you are, may the food you eat remind you of His body that was broken for each of us. May we also be intentional and relational in sharing the good news of Easter—generation to generation.

"He put a new song in my mouth, a hymn of praise to our God. Many will see and fear and put their trust in the Lord." Psalm 40:3 (NIV)

GIVING

"Honor the LORD with your wealth,
with the first fruits of all your crops."
Proverbs 3:9 (NIV)

I've read several books on Biblical stewardship and each author agrees on the following key for financial success: Understand that God owns it all. (Psalm 24:1)

We are merely stewards of God's property. This means God can take from us whatever He wants, whenever He wants it. Knowing God owns it all implies that every spending decision is a spiritual one. Stewardship cannot be faked. It's revealed in our checkbooks and calendars. Where we spend our money and our time reveals where our hearts really are. Biblical stewardship begins with God's tithe. As one preacher put it, "If you're not tithing, you're on your own!"

Avoid a consumptive lifestyle or as the saying goes, "Use it up; wear it out; make it do; or do without!"

1. Avoid the use of debt. Live within your means.
2. Maintain a savings program.
3. Set long-term goals. Financial maturity is being able to give up today's desires for future benefits.

As a young mom, I used to dread—dare I say, even hate— sermons on tithing and stewardship. Somebody always wanted more of my time and money and, in those days, there was never enough of either. Now I look back over the years and am amazed at God's faithfulness and provision. I can't explain how it happened, I only know it did. Somehow, God provided and met our every need—not our greed—but our need. As we first trusted Him with our tithe, He provided for our family every step of the way. There were free piano lessons, clothes, donated cars, college scholarships, extra jobs, fulfilled faith promise pledges, a wedding... the list goes on and on as gifts from God with no debt. Like the Psalmist David, I can truly say:

"I was young and now I am old, yet I have never seen the righteous forsaken or their children begging bread." (Psalm 37:25 NIV)

ENCOURAGE

*"The Son of man did not come to be served,
but to serve." Matthew 20:28 (NIV)*

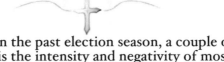

Reflecting upon the past election season, a couple of things struck me. The first is the intensity and negativity of most of the political advertisements for candidates of both political parties. The second is the appalling lack of character and integrity of many candidates. Finally, very few candidates really want to serve their constituents; rather they desire to be served by the elected office of which they seek.

Jesus provides a stark contrast to today's nasty politics. In the Kingdom of God or as Tim Keller calls it "the upside down kingdom,"[6] The King of Kings and Lord of Lords did not come to *be* served; He came *to* serve. How very different from today's leaders and our culture.

I heard a sermon once by a prominent pastor who thoughtfully characterized our current culture as:

- Overwhelmed with busyness - the average church member attends church 1.5 times monthly
- Over committed- to secondary things
- Overprotected - the age of adolescence has increased from age 18 post World War II to age 26 today
- Over rewarded - everyone gets a trophy whether or not he/she has earned it
- Over served

The pastor closed his remarks with a prayer that God would make us *over-comers*, rightly committed to knowing God and making Him known. We can fit into our culture's mold and be overwhelmed, over committed, overprotected, over rewarded, and over served OR we can, by God's grace, be over-comers who live counter culturally and seek to serve, rather than be served. The choice is ours and it's one that we make minute-by-minute and day-by-day.

Most of us probably don't have to look very far to find someone to serve today. In class, at the office, a boardroom, or on a practice field, there are those around us who need a kind and encouraging word, a smile, a meal, or a friend. Ask God to make you His servant today, to enable you to be His hands and feet, to bring the good news of the Gospel to a world that so desperately needs it.

ENCOURAGE

"Encourage one another and build each other up."
1 Thessalonians 5:11 (NIV)

Brucie hopped in the car one afternoon after work and excitedly waved a white piece of paper. "Mama! Mama! I got a good report."

I hesitated before I took the note from his hand. Usually a note for Brucie is a *bad* behavior report, not a good one. This time, however, the note was a report from the on-site dental clinic. The box with "healthy mouth" was checked as was the "we cleaned his teeth" treatment plan. At the bottom of the page were the words, "he was so great, so proud!" It's hard to imagine that six words could make my day, perhaps even my week. For most parents, dental visits can be trying for young children. For special needs parents and their children, routine tasks such as haircuts, vaccinations, and dental appointments are not just trying, but traumatic.

In the past, James Bruce would have to be partially sedated and then literally placed in a papoose with Velcro restraints in order to get his teeth cleaned. There have been times when his screams have challenged my ability to stay outside in the waiting room. I now marvel at how far he's come and how thankful I am for caring professionals willing to come to the UCP Center to make it easier for patients (especially autistic ones!) and their caregivers. I was overwhelmed and grateful that one person took the time to write the sentence affirming my disabled son and encouraging me.

I've thought a lot about those six words: "He was so great, so proud." I've considered the thoughtfulness of the one who wrote them. I've reflected on the excitement that James Bruce demonstrated as he waved his paper and happily said, "I got a good report!" Those six words are best summed up in one word: encouragement. The word, encouragement, literally means to "put courage into" or "come alongside."

Author John Maxwell has said, "Encouragement is the oxygen of the soul."[7]

Many of our Bible Bits have reflected on the negative aspects of our speech—bragging, complaining, careless and thoughtless words that steal and kill. Each one of these is a sin of commission, but what about the sins of omission? What about the times when God calls us to use our speech for the good of others and we fail to do so? Who in your life needs an encouraging word, a quick prayer, a note or card to express appreciation? What about speaking up for the rights of those

49

who can't speak for themselves? (Proverbs 31:8) God commands us to encourage one another, to build up one another, to pray for one another, and to teach one another. God gave us the gift of speech to use both for our good and for His glory.

Wherever you are today, look for someone to encourage and then just do it! We may never know the difference that an encouraging word or quick prayer can make for one who is struggling with low self-esteem, discouragement, fear, illness, or doubts. By God's grace, our words can be the Creator's tools for healing and helping folks instead of weapons for hurting others.

"Pleasant words are a honeycomb, sweet to the soul and healing to the bones." Proverbs 16:24 (NIV)

ENCOURAGE

*"Where is the one who has been born king of the Jews?
We saw his star in the east and have come
to worship him." Matthew 2:2 (NIV)*

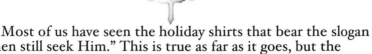

Most of us have seen the holiday shirts that bear the slogan "wise men still seek Him." This is true as far as it goes, but the problem seems to be that it doesn't go far enough. The original wise men didn't just seek Jesus; they didn't stop until they found Him.

We can learn several key points by looking at the passage in Matthew 2:1-12. First, their search was a *personal* search. Unlike Herod, they didn't send someone else to find Jesus. They left their country, families, and comfort zones to find Him themselves. The search was one with PURPOSE. They expected to find Him and they intended to worship Him when they found Him.

They were PREPARED to worship. Matthew 2:11 (NIV) says that, "they bowed down and worshipped Him. Then they opened their treasures and presented Him with gifts."

They PERSEVERED in their search. They didn't let temporary setbacks (like not finding him in the palace where one would expect to find a king) discourage them from ultimately finding Jesus.

Finally, after they found and worshipped Him, they demonstrated EXACT OBEDIENCE. Having been warned in a dream not to return to Herod, they returned to their country by another route (Matt 2:12). They chose to obey their heavenly King, rather than an earthly one.

For each of us, as we approach the New Year, may we be like the wise men. May we seek Jesus personally, with purpose and preparation. May we persevere not only in our search, but also in our worship and may our lives be a demonstration of exact obedience for God's glory.

ENCOURAGE

Encourage one another daily. Hebrews 3:13 (NIV)

An anonymous letter arrived in my sister's mailbox one day. She had experienced a bruising day at work, and was hurriedly opening her mail before she prepared supper. The letter stopped her in her tracks. Written by a member of her large adult couple's Sunday school class, the writer thanked her for taking the time and effort to teach. Not wanting to draw attention to herself, the woman simply said, "Thank you for continuing to encourage us to be the hands and feet of Jesus."

She also shared a few practical examples of how she and her family had tried to be the "hands and feet of Jesus" over the last few weeks: raking and bagging leaves for a single working mom, dropping off groceries to a woman battling cancer, writing a note of encouragement—all deeds done anonymously because the author struggles with issues of recognition and affirmation.

Jan and I both were touched as we realized that God can use anything that is placed in His hands. We were crying, however, by the end of the letter. The author asked Jan to teach on how to study your Bible. She asked, "How do you stay motivated to keep studying?" She also went on to say that she had read the Bible as a child, but now she wasn't sure where or how to begin.

We both were shaken. Our good works, no matter how well intentioned they are, should never be a substitute for cultivating our relationship with Jesus. Our good works are to be an *overflow* of that relationship rather than a *substitute*. Jesus said, "Let your light shine before men in such a way that they may see your good works and glorify your Father who is in heaven." (Matthew 5:16 ESV)

Yes, He expects good works, but only after the light within us—Jesus, Himself—shines brightly. His light should always come first. The result is that God gets the glory, both from our relationship with Jesus and the good works that follow. However, *doing* is never a substitute for *being*.

As for what motivates one to keep studying, Jeremiah said it best: "When your words came, I ate them; they were my joy and my heart's delight, for I bear your name." Jeremiah 15:16 (NIV)

ENCOURAGE

"Speak up for those who cannot speak for themselves, for the rights of all who are destitute. Speak up and judge fairly; defend the rights of the poor and needy." Proverbs 31:8-9 (NIV)

Monday was James Bruce's 26th birthday but no matter how much I try to emotionally prepare myself, his birthday is always difficult for me. This year was no different as I reflected on the day he was born and how I'd always wanted, for as long as I could remember, a little boy named Bruce. We had no way of knowing on February 1, 1984, how dramatically our lives would be impacted by James Bruce's birth.

At first, it was the usual additional chores, laundry, time and budget constraints of having three kids under four-years-old. Our lives, however, quickly became a blur of sleepless nights, growing fears, and endless doctor visits trying to figure out what was wrong with him. James Bruce was three when he was diagnosed with mild mental deficiency; five when we had the genetics done that showed he has an anomaly on chromosome 15 (responsible for neurological development); and nine when he was diagnosed with autism.

In 1989, God gave me a very special verse of Scripture, "I will give you treasures of darkness and hidden wealth of secret places in order that you will know that I am the Lord your God who calls you by your name." (Isaiah 45:3 NAS) At the time, my life was very dark and I couldn't imagine anything being good, much less valuable. Gradually, God began to show me that "treasures of darkness" are those invaluable life lessons that we learn in pain and adversity that we'd never learn if life were easy and comfortable. One of my "treasures" has been learning to speak up for those who can't speak for themselves and to literally be a voice for those who don't have one.

There are dark times in everyone's lives, but we don't have to stay in the dark. We can choose to walk out into the light. Consider the Gentile prostitute, Rahab, who chose faith and God when she provided protection, provision, and encouragement for the Israeli spies prior to the battle of Jericho. You can read her story for yourself in Joshua chapters two and six, but this prostitute with a dark past eventually makes it into the Hebrews 11 Hall of Fame for the Faithful. She's commended for her faith in Hebrews 11 and for her works in James 2. More than this, however, she is one of four women named in the genealogy of Jesus in Matthew 1:5. Rahab serves as an encouragement and example for all of us who have a past.

ENCOURAGE

✝

God, in His infinite wisdom, made the seasons of cold and heat, summer and winter, seedtime and harvest. (Genesis 8:22) I was reminded of His creativity as we hiked up the trail to Klingman's Dome (the highest point in Tennessee) in the Smoky Mountains National Forest. It wasn't just the majesty of the mountains and the beauty of the valleys; it was the diversity of people and cultures that surrounded us. Everyone had come with one goal in mind—making it to the top.

Three times on the steep climb to the top, James Bruce encouraged me by saying, "We can make it," and he was right—make it we did. That encouragement reminded me of the Hebrews 11 Hall of Fame for the Faithful—that great cloud of witnesses who have gone before us. They encourage us to keep going, never give up, fix our eyes on Jesus, and finish well.

Those timely lessons were gentle reminders to enjoy the summer and our time spent together as a family—learning from each other and being grateful to the Creator who knew that both summer and winter are vitally necessary for the growth and balance of His children.

May God bless you with His peace and His presence this season.

ENCOURAGE

"Get rid of all bitterness, rage, and anger."
Ephesians 4:31 (NIV)

In our family, we have reunions with extended family every summer. In preparation for one of these events, I was doing some deep cleaning—knocking down cobwebs and wiping over baseboards. In doing so, I got a tiny splinter in my finger. It didn't bother me too much the first few days. Oh, I knew it was there, but I kept delaying getting the splinter out. By Sunday night, however, it was a different story. My index finger was red and angry looking. The splinter was walled off and a little swollen. It hurt to use my finger. In short, I couldn't wait to get the thing out. Once removed, I applied some hydrogen peroxide to the small wound and by Monday morning, my finger was almost back to normal.

That's a little snapshot of what bitterness, anger, and rage can do in our hearts. At first, we may know something is wrong, but we push it aside and don't deal with it. God says to get rid of it—remove it. Don't hang on to it or allow it to fester. Instead of denial, we're to actively rid ourselves of anything that would allow bitterness to grow unchecked.

So what about it? Is there any unresolved situation in your life that needs to be dealt with? Do you need to forgive someone for a past offense? Do you need to ask someone's forgiveness?

Most of us practice avoidance or denial, but God wants us to confront our pain and get rid of it at its source. Just as my finger couldn't heal until the splinter was removed, so my heart, soul, and mind won't rest until, by God's grace, I get rid of anything that causes bitterness, rage or anger.

The Nike® people got it right with their ad slogan, Just do it!®

ENCOURAGE

Most of us don't have little wooden or carved idols in our homes, cars or purses. All of us, however, have things in our lives that sometimes takes God's rightful first place in our lives. Perhaps it's a job, material possessions, pleasure, or even our children, but God is very concerned that we don't cling, hold on to, or refuse to be separated from anyone or anything other than Himself.

When we fail to forgive somebody, refuse to give up attitudes of anger and bitterness, or stubbornly cling to some bad habits—something else consumes our emotions, energy, focus, and passion. God's word is clear—when we do this, we also forfeit or give up His grace that could have been our own. Instead of experiencing His healing, strength, and sufficiency, we insist on our right to be angry, bitter, and unforgiving.

We have a choice and decisions always have consequences. May we, like Joshua, choose to serve the LORD.

ENCOURAGE

*"Now finish the work, so that your eager willingness
to do it may be matched by your completion of it,
according to your means." 2 Cor 8:11 (NIV)*

"Finish well." That's always been the motto around our house. Whether it's baseball, a high school career, AP physics class, or the Relay for Life drive, we keep challenging our high school senior, Daniel, to finish well. Of the almost 400 characters in the Bible, only 67 finished well. Even Solomon, the wisest man who ever lived, was among those who didn't finish well.

The question is "Why?" Why do eager folks who start with such great promise fail to finish well? The Apostle Paul knew about finishing well and he wanted to impart his knowledge to others. Prior to Paul's death and in his final written letter to Timothy, he cited distraction, disqualification, and discouragement as three obstacles to overcome in order to finish well. (2 Timothy 2:4-6)

With all of the hoopla surrounding Daniel's high school graduation—including prom, summer jobs, and college plans—it's easy to get distracted from the primary task at hand. In the recently completed winter Olympics, one highly regarded skier who was expected to medal in at least four events, failed to medal in any event because he skied outside the course. As a result, he was disqualified and failed to finish at all. Discouragement and insecurity can also influence our outcome by causing us to quit or falter—in a marriage, a sport, a job, or even a friendship. We lose perspective by focusing on our circumstances instead of our God.

So how are you finishing? What can you do to finish well in whatever endeavor God has placed before you? Throughout our lives, it takes discipline to live in the moment—the here and now. While we can plan for the future, God wants us to live in the present and in His presence. We have to daily (sometimes hourly and minute-by-minute) discipline our emotions and do our "next thing"—whatever it is.

May we all be like Paul who was able to say:
"I have finished the course." 2 Timothy 4:7 (NAS)

SHARING FAITH

"Then Philip...told him the good news about Jesus."
Acts 8:35 (NIV)

A headline in the local paper read, "Life lived, not life invented."[8] The article focused on the life, career, and legacy of 92-year-old, Kathryn Tucker Windham, a nationally acclaimed storyteller who recently died. Pulitzer Prize author Rick Bragg called her an "authentic treasure."

"She had that storyteller's front-porch delivery," said Bragg. "It didn't matter whether she was speaking into a microphone, a telephone, or to a banquet room full of people, she was speaking about life lived, not life invented. That's a big difference."

Windham often used her own life experiences to provide her listeners with a powerful link to the past and to encourage others to share their own stories. Before her death, Windham shared her thoughts about the art of storytelling.

"I began to realize that what we needed to be telling are stories about our own families, about people we know and love and care about. That's how you keep the memories alive. You don't forget the people you love when you tell stories about them and tell new generations these stories about them."

Windham lamented the loss of storytelling in families and chalked this loss up to many factors, including modern day conveniences like air-conditioning. "It moved people off the front porch and into the house to watch television," she explained. Another factor was the disappearance of country stores ("People would come and go and tell stories and I don't hear them telling stories in any Wal-Mart"). The same could be said of funeral homes. Windham said, "When people died, you used to go to their homes and sit up with the dead. Different people would come in and tell stories about the dead person. These were wonderful stories told all during the night, but we don't do that anymore."

Windham is no longer around to tell her stories, but her legacy lives on in the form of encouragement to others to share their own stories. She said, "And do it with all your heart. Treat the people as if they're the most important audience in the world, because for that moment—they are."

None of my stories will change anyone's life, but God's story—of grace, love, and redemption—once told and received, can change anyone's life.

A good story is real, raw, and redemptive—and this is the good news of Jesus—the greatest story ever told.

SHARING FAITH

*"The things that you have heard me say in the presence of
many witnesses entrust to reliable men who will also
be qualified to teach others." 2 Timothy 2:2 (NIV)*

One afternoon while walking at a high school track, I witnessed four young men practicing their sprints and baton transfers. Again and again, they sprinted and transferred. With each practice, I watched the lead runner speed around the track while awaiting the arrival of another runner on his team. The goal of the second team runner was to position himself side-by-side with the lead runner so a baton exchange could be attempted while both were running.

Watching them, I was struck by how intentional and relational the whole process was. It took each athlete running his leg of the race for all of the young men to finish. If one man failed to transfer the baton, the team was disqualified and the race was run in vain. The key to the whole race hinged on how well the baton transfer occurred.

Much like the relay runners, God intends for us to transfer His truth generation to generation intentionally and relationally through our families, churches, and life-on-life discipleship. We are always supposed to point the next generation to Him, telling them both who He is and what He has done in our lives. The transfer of truth is never limited to just one generation. In God's economy and by His design, four generations are impacted.

Paul instructed Timothy to teach reliable men who in turn could teach others. Paul the principal leader instructed Timothy the proven leader who in turn taught reliable men (potential leaders) who taught others (possible leaders). The same pattern is true throughout the Bible (Psalm 78, Psalm 145, Titus 2) for families and church communities.

Intentional and relational are two keys to the successful transfer of truth to the next generation. We must be committed to intentionally and purposefully knowing God ourselves and making Him known to others. Then we must win the right to be heard by being relational. Someone once said, "Rules without a relationship equals rebellion."

So what about you? How well do you know God personally? Are you intentionally and relationally making Him known to others? Whose life or lives could be eternally impacted by your life? God never meant for us to sit, soak, and sour, but He always means for us to sit, soak and GO tell somebody else about Jesus.

SHARING FAITH

"He who refreshes others will himself be refreshed."
Proverbs 11:25 (NIV)

I have a friend who invests her life and time in cultivating relationships and serving others. One Sunday afternoon found me accompanying her to the county jail with two other friends from our church. I'm still not exactly sure how I got there, or even why. She had never specifically asked me to go with her, but somehow I needed to see for myself what motivates her to keep going every third Sunday of each month.

The rain was pouring and the weather was cold and penetrating, a perfect Sunday nap day. We chatted the whole car ride and before I knew it, we were there. Once inside the jail complex, my stomach was doing little flip-flops as I wondered what might be on the other side of the steel doors. We signed in the visitor book and my friend led the way. My plan was to watch, listen, observe, pray, and get out safely.

I've never been to a jail before, so I was surprised to see that there were no bars. This jail is state of the art with pressurized sliding gray metal doors. In fact, everything was gray: the concrete blocks, the stainless steel tables, the walls, the floors, and the doors. Once we got to our pod, there were 15 women prisoners housed there. Seven of them responded to our invitation to "come to church."

As we gathered around the steel lunch table, I was surprised to see that all but one of the women had a Bible. All of us were a little unsure of how to proceed, but we sat down and each woman shared her first name. My friend asked if anyone had a favorite song that we could sing. We finally settled on *Jesus Loves Me*. I was surprised and comforted at the clarity, truth, and strength displayed in the lyrics:

> "Jesus loves me this I know,
> For the Bible tells me so.
> Little ones to Him belong.
> They are weak but He is strong.
> Yes, Jesus loves me."

Afterward we sang, *Jesus Loves the Little Children,* and *He's Got the Whole World in His Hands.* In my mind, I was transported back to Mrs. Maynard's four-year-old Sunday school class. This is where I first learned these songs. Never in my wildest dreams would I have imagined myself singing them in a jail.

As we finished singing, my friend commented that music could lift our soul to God. When she asked if anyone had something to share, I told them about James Bruce's mental deficiency and autism, his love of music, and how God has used him in ways I could never have dreamed. We talked about brokenness; how God can use the pieces of our lives to feed a hungry and needy world. Just as He used broken loaves to feed 5,000, so He takes the pieces of our lives and uses them for our good and for His glory if we give them to Him. The women seemed to identify with brokenness and pieces.

On the way back, I was surprised to feel refreshed and energized, eager to go again, thankful for the experience and expectant that God would bear fruit, not only in their lives, but in mine. God never asks us for things we don't have, but He always asks, "What do you have?" All of us have something to give that He can use. When we in obedience give what we have, He blesses and uses both the giver and the gift. The question is: Will we give it to him?

"It is more blessed to give than to receive." Acts 20:35

SHARING FAITH

"I am the way, the truth, and the life."
John 14:6 (NIV)

It happens almost daily. On my way through the corridors and crosswalks at the hospital, I find people at an intersection, looking around helplessly, often with a map or directions, trying to decide which way to go. No matter what time of day—coming in to work in the morning, going to meetings or lunch, or leaving in the afternoon—I can almost always find someone who needs help getting to the right place. I used to ask, "Do you need help?" Most of the time there would be a faint smile, a half-hearted "I think I can do this by myself," and then a lengthy response detailing where, what, or who they were trying to find.

Lately, in order to save time, I've simply asked, "Are you lost?" The response is usually a quick "Yes." It seems that acknowledging this fact is the first step in getting yourself pointed in the right direction.

It struck me driving home the other day that what is true in the physical world is also certainly true in the spiritual realm. Every day, if I choose to look, I come across folks who have lost their way. They may not physically be standing at an intersection trying to determine the right course, but they are at a crossroads, nonetheless. Confusion, doubt, anger, bitterness, frustration, hopelessness, are all signs that someone needs help in finding the One who declared Himself to be not A way, but THE Way. The issue then becomes: How willing am I to show the Way to them? Am I as quick to point them to Jesus, as I am to get them to the parking deck?

So what about you? Are you lost or simply having trouble finding your way? Jesus—the Way, the Truth and the Life—came to seek and to save that which was lost. (Luke 19:10) We, as His followers, should go and do likewise.

SHARING FAITH

"And the house was filled with the fragrance of the perfume."
John 12:3 (NIV)

My daughter, Meredith, unexpectedly sent me a beautiful cut-flower arrangement to my office one day. At first, I kept my office door closed, but soon the fragrance from the lilies was overpowering. The heady scent made a difference in the room. I opened the door and soon people from all over our floor were following the pungent smell to see the flowers.

Today's verse describes another very generous and unexpected gift. After Jesus raised Lazarus from the dead, a few days later Lazarus' sister Mary poured out a pint of very expensive perfume onto Jesus and wiped His feet with her hair.

The house was filled with the perfume's fragrance. Mary received harsh criticism from Judas for her extravagant gift. He wondered why the perfume hadn't been sold and the money given to the poor. Jesus replied, "Leave her alone...she has done what she could." (Mark 14:6-8)

Where others saw waste, Jesus saw worship. Where others dished out criticism and condemnation, Jesus extended reward and recognition. Jesus acknowledged Mary's gratitude, love, and sacrificial giving. She intentionally counted the cost and chose Christ.

Paul in 2 Corinthians 2:14 (NIV) says that, "God who always leads us in triumphant procession in Christ and through us spreads everywhere the fragrance of the knowledge of Him." Just as Meredith's lilies led folks to my office, so our lives should lead people to Christ. God somehow chooses to use us to share the good news of the gospel of Christ. So how's your fragrance? Does it fill your home, your office, your community, and your heart? When others look at your life, do they ask what makes the difference? May all of our lives be "a fragrant offering, an acceptable sacrifice, pleasing to God." Philippians 4:18 (NIV)

SHARING FAITH

*"The people who know their God will display strength
and take action." Daniel 11:32 (NAS)*

My mentor recently died of lung cancer. Barbara was an older woman who had been married for 50 plus years, raised three children, influenced ten grandchildren, and mentored countless younger women. If you asked me to describe her in one word, it would be "strength." When she retired, it took two full-time and two part-time folks to do what she had previously done in 20 hours per week.

I learned from her that you should use what you have and not worry about what you don't have. Thus, we used her good china and crystal for potluck dinners. She opened her home to missionaries and college students. Her kids and grandkids were scattered across the country making it difficult to get together on holidays. She cooked anyhow, and invited others without a family to come to her feast.

Outside of my parents and family, Barbara is one of three people to help shape my perspective and worldview. In one of her last emails, she detailed her latest medical procedure and also sent her instructions on intentional grand-mothering tips.

When Barb could no longer go to church to teach women, she taught them in her home. She kept teaching until God called her home. I've thought a lot about her the last week. She taught me these life lessons:

1. Teach what you've been taught.
2. Be intentional in cultivating relationships.
3. Open both your heart and your home and share it with others.
4. Hospitality is making folks feel welcome, wanted, and worth the trouble.
5. Invest your life, don't just spend it.
6. Find intentional ways to grandparent from afar if necessary. (She would read books on tape, make quilts, Thanksgiving and Christmas decorations or costumes, and send packages—anything to connect to her grandchildren.)
7. No pity-parties are allowed.
8. Have your tools ready and God will find you work. (She always had three women that she would disciple. If one married or moved, she would pray and God would send her another one to "grow up in Jesus.")

"A woman who fears the Lord, she shall be praised."
Proverbs 31:30 (NAS)

SHARING FAITH

"They will be called oaks of righteousness, a planting of the Lord, for the display of His splendor." Isaiah 61:3 (NIV)

Some time ago, there were news reports detailing a national airline's attempts at political correctness. It seemed that during in-flight movies, any reference to God, except for profanity, was bleeped out. One passenger angrily complained about the airline's decision-making process. At the heart of the matter was an attempt to *not* offend anyone who didn't believe in God. No one stopped to consider that those who *DO* believe in God would be offended.

It seemed that this airline was not the only business to strike out references to God. News reports from the 2007 NFL Super Bowl made much ado about Coach Tony Dungy being the first African-American head coach to lead his team to the Super Bowl. Watching Coach Dungy's press interviews after the game, I counted at least five times where he said he was proud to be the first African-American coach to win a Super Bowl, but he considered it more important that he was a man of faith in God. He went on to say that, he and Coach Lovie Smith, head coach of the Chicago Bears, are both men of faith. They both showed that you could win doing things "the right way."

I never saw Coach Dungy's remarks quoted by the AP in the Monday paper. Yet his life still stands as a testimony to the value of knowing Christ. He demonstrated faith and courage both on and off the football field. His 21-year-old son committed suicide shortly after his win, but Coach Dungy's testimony held firm. He has spoken out about his faith whenever the opportunity has arisen.

God wants each of our lives to be living testimonies to the value of knowing Him. If someone bleeped out your verbal references to God, would others still be able to see the difference that knowing Christ makes? God wants our lives to tell His story. Few of us will win a Super Bowl, but we can, by God's grace and Spirit, live lives that point men and women to Jesus.

> "It is no use walking anywhere to preach unless our walking is our preaching." -St. Francis of Assisi

SHARING FAITH

"I am not ashamed of the gospel."
Romans 1:16 (NIV)

James Bruce and I walked in our church lobby one Sunday morning and were greeted by Benjamin, a young man with Down's syndrome. Benjamin is in his late twenties and is very high functioning for an adult with a disability. He has impeccable manners and is always sharply dressed. His dad is a local businessman who owns a restaurant and you can tell that manners have been a big part of Benjamin's training. Benjamin greeted us warmly and asked me if I wanted him to take James Bruce to his Special Ones class. I said, "No, but thanks. We're going to the service for a while so James Bruce can listen to the music and then we'll get him to his class." Benjamin's face fell just a bit, but he asked James Bruce for a hug. JB allowed a half-hug and we went on to church.

That night I saw Benjamin again at church. This time he was with some family members. I went to thank him for his extraordinary kindness to James Bruce. He surprised me once again with his manners and presence.

"I'd like to present my family," he said. One-by-one, he introduced them—a brother-in-law, a niece, and a sister. The family members looked a little embarrassed, but I shook hands with each one and commended Benjamin once again for his helpfulness, manners, and kindness.

Benjamin didn't waste any time before asking me, "Do you know why I am different?"

I thought for a moment, unsure of how to respond. Finally, I just asked him why he thought he was different.

Again, Benjamin didn't hesitate. "I'm different because I have Jesus Christ in my heart and He makes the difference in my life. He will make the difference in anyone's life if you believe in Him."

Surprised and relieved, I agreed and returned to our seats. Later when I told the Special Ones Director about the incident, she laughed. "Benjamin loves to tell people about Jesus. Last year he flew to China with his Dad on some business project. As they were boarding the plane, the pilots let Benjamin say something to the passengers over the intercom. They expected him to say something like 'testing' or 'have a good flight.' Much to their surprise, Benjamin told all of the passengers not to worry, that God was the real pilot of the plane, and He would deliver them all safely."

Recently, I've thought a lot about Benjamin's boldness. Actually, I've prayed to be more like him—confident, sure of what I believe, and not worried about what other people think or whether or not I'm politically correct. Benjamin is teaching me something about transparency, authenticity, and being prepared to make a defense for the hope that is in me. May we all be like Benjamin—unashamed of the gospel and able to clearly say, "Jesus Christ is the reason that I'm different."

"I am not ashamed, because I know whom I have believed."
2 Timothy 1:12 (NAS)

GRACE

Most of us expect God to give us spiritual insight when we're sitting in church listening to a sermon or studying our daily devotional or Bible, but sometimes God gives us "gold nuggets" in the ordinary events of daily living. This is what happened to me one morning at work.

An outside auditor had scheduled an audit for Tuesday morning. Monday afternoon I received a call from him reminding me to have all of the requested information available. I assured him that the information was already pulled and then asked, "Do you know where you're going or do you need directions?"

He quickly rattled off the address for the clinic and said he knew where to go. "It's a big building and the pharmacy is on the second floor," I offered. He didn't respond except to say that the audit would begin promptly at 8:30 a.m.

Tuesday morning at 8:30 found me in the ambulatory manager's office with both of us waiting for the auditor. After 20 minutes, I decided to return to my office and leave the audit information with the other manager. "If he shows up, call me," I said as I left for the two-block walk back to my office.

As I unlocked my office door, my telephone was ringing. When I answered, I was confronted with an angry, impatient voice who demanded, "Where are you and why aren't you here?"

I guess it didn't help that I started laughing as I replied, "I'm in my office. The real question is, where are you?"

It turned out that the poor guy was indeed lost in the maze of buildings and concourses in the downtown area. He wasn't even sure what floor he was on. I instructed him to find the coffee shop on the second floor and wait on a nearby bench until I could come and retrieve him.

I calmly hummed most of the two-block walk over to the North Pavilion as I remembered John Newton's famous line from Amazing Grace, "I once was lost but now am found." Those words took on fresh meaning as soon as I saw the bewildered, lost auditor. He was sitting on a bench with his head in his hands looking pretty miserable. He made matters worse by blaming everyone else for his lateness. The same pride, which prevented him from accepting directions, prevented him from acknowledging his own folly.

It struck me that his key to "being found" was admitting he was lost. The same principle is true for us spiritually. Until we admit we're helpless, hopeless, and in need of a Savior, we can't be found. The minute we admit we're lost on our own and need His help, we find that help—and grace—is present. John Newton never got over Amazing Grace and neither should we.

So what about you? Are you lost or have you been found by Jesus? Don't let your pride or anything else keep you from admitting your need to be found by and in Jesus.

GRACE

"If anyone is in Christ, he is a new creation;
the old has gone, the new has come!"
2 Corinthians 5:17(NIV)

✝

I first met him when he was four-years-old. He was the cutest kid in the church nursery. David had dark eyes and hair, an infectious laugh, and a winsome personality. Bruce and I had just moved to the small community. Meredith was an infant, just a few-weeks-old, and we were visiting churches trying to find a new church home. David's parents unexpectedly invited us to their farm home for lunch afterward. We shared a rainy Sunday afternoon with ham sandwiches and vegetable soup, fellowship, laughter, and the beginning of a lifelong friendship.

Through the years I kept up with David's parents. I knew that David struggled to find himself. His parents struggled to parent him, first as a teenager and then as an adult. Every Christmas card ended with the plea, "Please pray for David." Sometimes God would inexplicably bring him to my mind and heart, but mainly when I cleaned the boys' bathroom. On my knees, scrubbing a tub, I would pray for David to come home, not only to his parents, but to God.

His letter and picture arrived in my mailbox today. It began: "As a Christian, one of the most exciting things is to be informed of the result of answered prayer. Many of you know about the life I have led and have been a part of a mighty prayer team protecting me not only from outside influences, but from myself as well."

The letter went on to detail truthfully his life of rebellion, alcohol, drug abuse, promiscuity, arrests, rehab, and eventually hitting rock bottom. It also detailed his prayer for God to take control of his life, his subsequent entry into a rehab program, and his current ministry to the White Swan Indians on the Yakima Reservation in Wapato, Washington. David closed his letter by thanking me for past prayers and asking me to pray once again for God's direction in his life. David's serene expression in his picture confirmed what I already know: He *is* home.

It was a "holy ground" moment in my kitchen as I read his letter twice. Two verses quickly came to mind, "Gather up the fragments that remain, so that nothing is lost." (John 6:12 NKJV) and "I will restore to you the years the locusts have eaten." (Joel 2:25 NKJV) Only God can do this. Only God can use our mistakes and messes and turn our ashes into something beautiful for His glory. The good news is that He can and He does do just that if we let Him.

GRACE

"And the God of all grace...will himself restore you
and make you strong, firm, and steadfast."
1 Peter 5:10 (NIV)

In my devotional time I came to a verse in Proverbs that sent me to cross-reference today's verse. The words literally jumped off of the page and into my heart. I quickly wrote them down in my journal, so grateful to have a definite "sacred echo" to mull over throughout the day. All day I considered the words "God himself will make you strong, firm, and steadfast." I decided that this verse would be my 2011 prayer verse for our family. I found comfort and joy in the promise that the God of all grace would Himself make us strong, firm and steadfast.

Little did I know yesterday morning how much I would need those words last night. James Bruce and I had gone to the evening worship service. Bruce was still recovering from only five hours of sleep following Friday night's out-of-town football game. One of the team buses had broken down. A new bus had to be dispatched, and Bruce got home at 3:00 a.m. on Saturday morning.

The sermon had just begun when my cell phone started vibrating. At first I was irritated until I saw who was calling. The Special Ones coordinator was trying to reach me. I instantly knew that James Bruce was having a seizure. I grabbed my things and left the sanctuary running. By the time I arrived, the seizure was past the four-minute-mark. The violent seizure kept going and a medical emergency alert was initiated. In just moments, we had five doctors on the scene and four praying pastors in the hallway. One of the doctors said we needed to get him to the hospital, so we called 911 and landed at the closest ER. James Bruce had another seizure enroute.

About 2 a.m. this morning, I got my Bible out to again read today's verse. By then all I could remember was "God Himself... strong, firm, steadfast." As I read the verse, I found new meaning in the words I had previously missed. I Peter 5:10 (NIV) reads:

> "And the God of all grace, who called you to his eternal glory in Christ, after you have suffered a little while, will himself restore you and make you strong, firm and steadfast."

Suddenly, I realized that the strong, firm, and steadfast that each of us is promised in this verse does not come until AFTER the suffering. We are also assured that God Himself will provide these things.

Elisabeth Elliot's definition of suffering is the best one that I know. She writes, "Suffering is having what you don't want or wanting what you don't have."[9] I definitely don't want seizures for James Bruce, and I certainly do not enjoy watching my child suffer. Yet, I know that God still reigns and rules and that He CAN and WILL use all of this for our good and for His glory. I don't know the HOW, but I absolutely know the WHO—the God of all grace.

"Spread your protection over them." Psalm 5:11 (NIV)

"And He shall be the stability of your times, a wealth of wisdom, salvation, and knowledge; the fear of the Lord is the key to this treasure." Isaiah 33:6 (NAS)

GRACE

"But when, he the Spirit of truth comes, he will guide you into all truth."
John 16:13 (NIV)

The Evans family was headed to Washington, D.C. A friend of mine had suggested to me that I call our Congressman's office staff to request a tour of our nation's capital. We scheduled our tour for the last day of our trip. I had been in a three-day business conference and missed much of the sight seeing that Bruce and Daniel had experienced.

We were excited about the tour, but none of us really knew what we were in for. We were surprised that one of Daniel's good friends, Elliott, was interning there and would be our tour guide for the day.

Elliott began our tour by taking us underground through a maze of tunnels. He informed us that because we'd scheduled the tour through our Congressman's office, we'd be able to avoid some of the long lines and public entrances. We still had to go through multiple security checks, but we rode a mini-train that quickly got us from the Rayburn Building to the Capital. Elliott knew exactly where to go and how to get there. Additionally, he had his staff identification badge that allowed access to certain restricted places. Elliott knew which exhibits to point out, the fascinating history of each room, and how to get us in multiple venues. I found myself hanging on to Elliott's arm when we got in crowds. I was afraid of losing him and not knowing *where* to go or *what* to do.

At the beginning of our tour, I was pretty anxious because I was in totally unfamiliar territory. As we went along, however, I began to relax because Elliott knew the way, not just physically, but logistically. By the end of our tour, I decided that having a personal guide who knew the way and showed it to me was the best way to travel.

We were almost finished with our tour when it hit me. Elliott's guidance provided safety, security, and gave personal meaning and insight into our capital journey. The Holy Spirit does the same thing, plus so much more on our Christian journey. Later, in the airport terminal, my capital tour intersected with the following excerpt from David Platt's best-seller book, *Radical*.

> "The Holy Spirit is the Comforter, the Helper, the Guide, the very presence of God living in you. The great promise of God in prayer is this: We ask God for the gift—He gives us the Giver. We ask God for the supply and He gives us the Source. We ask God for the money and He doesn't give us

cash; instead, so to speak, He gives us the bank... He delights in giving us Himself... The resources of heaven are ready and waiting for the people of God who desire to make much of him in this world."[16]

Thanks to Elliott and my capital tour, I have a much better understanding of both the importance and function of a personal guide. I understand better what Jesus meant when He said, "I am the way, the truth, and the life." (John 14:6) Jesus made the way to God when He died on the cross and paid the penalty for my sin. He made the way, knew the way, and shows the way to God because He IS the way.

Wherever you are today, on whatever road you're traveling, if you know Jesus, you're never alone—for He IS with you.

Enjoy His grace—extend His glory!

GRACE

*"He put a new song in my mouth, a hymn of praise to our God.
Many will see and fear and put their trust in the Lord."*
Psalm 40:3 (NIV)

Two weeks ago my sister gave me a ride home from a cousin's wedding. She had a new CD playing that I enjoyed so much that I went and bought one for myself. Entitled *Rescue*, it's by a group called Newsong. Suddenly, everywhere I turned in my Bible last week, I found references to the words "new song."

The first recorded song in the Bible was Moses' song in Exodus 15. It described God's miraculous deliverance of Israel from Egypt via the Red Sea. David had a new song in 2 Samuel 22:1 when God delivered him from King Saul. Deborah and Miriam also have recorded songs of deliverance. The Psalms, of course, are actually songs. I was most surprised to find another new song in Revelation 5 and 15. There the saints in heaven have a new song to the Lamb of God:

> "Worthy is the Lamb, who was slain,
> to receive power and wealth and wisdom and strength
> and honor and glory and praise!" (Rev 5:12 NIV)

All of the references to "new songs" in the Bible celebrate God's deliverance. It occurred to me this week, that God's gift was not just the victory, but also the song. Perhaps God knew that it would be easier to memorize and recount the historic details in the form of a song rather than the text from a book. Maybe He knew that remembering the tune would in fact help us to remember the lyrics. Regardless, I am grateful for both His deliverance and the gift of music.

My favorite song on the "Rescue" album is entitled "Before the Day."[1] The singer describes his quiet time as "going steady with EDDY." He says that a quiet time is best done Early, Daily, Diligently, and Yieldingly (EDDY). That's a great way to remember the how-to's of a quiet time—early, daily, diligently, and yielding. In the stillness of the morning, when we come to God with purposeful expectation, He somehow gives each of us a new song, not just for our day, but for our lives. Our prayer should be that it would be His song and not our own.

So how's your singing? All of us should have our own new song about God's deliverance in life. If it has been a while since you've felt His music or presence, try going "steady with EDDY."

God will meet you there and give you a song to sing.

"You surround me with songs of deliverance." Psalm 32:7 (NIV)

GRACE

"the God of all grace."
1 Peter 5:10 (NIV)

My sacred echo this week has been the word "grace" and God has given me plenty of opportunities to both extend and receive grace. What I'm finding out about me is that I'm much more willing to receive grace than I am at extending it. Wednesday morning was a good God given test to see how well I understood the grace concept. In my Bible study, I latched onto Paul's opening notes in his final letter to Timothy: "fan into flame the gift of God." (2 Timothy 1:6 NIV) I looked up the English word "gift" and discovered that the Greek word "charisma" really means "gift of grace, undeserved benefit." Using this definition, it's easier to see that the gift of God is in fact, the gift of His grace.

I was still reflecting on the paradigm that "God's gift = God's grace" as I was packing our lunches. We were running a little bit late, and I was hurrying trying to finish our morning pre-work, out-the-door preparations when I realized that I hadn't fixed Brucie's daily travel mug of coffee. Quickly I heated his coffee in the microwave, but in my haste, spilled most of the coffee on the stove and kitchen counter top. Frustrated with both the mess and delay, I moaned, "Ohhh!" James Bruce was just coming through the kitchen, saw the mess, and quickly said, "That's OK Mama. I please forgive you!"

He totally disarmed me with his generous word of grace. I started laughing, even as I cleaned up my mess. I marveled at both James Bruce's timing and God's sense of humor. With both love and gentleness, God gave me a real life lesson in what grace is and what it looks like... an undeserved, unmerited "I please forgive you."

All of us have messes and stresses in our lives that require God's gifts of grace. Those grace gifts include patience, forgiveness, gentleness, laughter and an ability to not take ourselves too seriously. God desires that we be men and women who not only receive grace, but who also extend grace to others.

Wherever you are today, ask God to make you more like Stephen, the first Christian martyr, who is described as "a man full of God's grace and power." (Acts 6:8) We can't be full of God's grace and full of ourselves at the same time, but when we're full of God's grace, God's glory is reflected in our lives.

May all of us be people who are full of God's grace for God's glory.

RELATIONSHIP

"She girds her arms with strength."
Proverbs 31:17 (NIV)

Last Friday I met a friend at the park. She is a young mom who has a three-year-old daughter and is expecting her second child. We meet a couple of times each month to walk and talk, or sometimes just to talk. It's a learning process for both of us, but the reality is that I learn more from her than she does from me. It helps me remember just how short, and how hard the child-rearing process can be.

It was a beautiful day and my friend's three-year-old daughter, Ella Clae, joined us for our walk. Actually, Ella Clae, sat in a stroller and rode while we walked. Eventually we found our way to a park bench by the children's playground equipment. Ella Clae went up the ladder steps and down the various slides, happily playing and entertaining herself. She soon wanted to try the rings and realized that she needed some help.

I went over and coaxed her into letting me help her. She was hesitant at first, but soon enough reached out to grab hold of a ring when I assured her that I wouldn't let her fall. Together we crossed the distance between the two ladders, one ring at a time. She wanted to repeat the whole process, and this time we did it faster and more confidently.

Today's verse from Proverbs, were the words that kept coming to my mind and heart as Ella Clae laughingly moved from one ring to the next. Not only was Ella Clae building physical strength by exercising, she was building other skills as well. Over the course of the hour that we were together, Ella Clae's mom reminded her to take turns, be friendly to others, and to say "thank you" and "yes ma'am." In this brief span of time so many teaching opportunities presented themselves that will serve Ella Clae well throughout her lifetime. That's the way God designed the transfer of truth—one generation to the next.

Ella Clae wasn't the only one learning lessons that day. My focus words are "intentional" and "relational." I learned a lot about being intentional and relational simply by watching my friend with her daughter. Most of the teaching and learning that happened occurred in the ordinary moments of the day as a mother corrected her child when needed, encouraged her when she attempted something new, and loved and laughed with her as they spent time together. Being intentional and relational wasn't just a task on my friend's to do list; it was a byproduct of her affection for her daughter.

This is the kind of relationship God desires with each of us, His children. He wants us to desire to spend time with Him, listening to Him and learning from Him. God wants us to delight in being with Him; as we spend time with God, His joy becomes our strength. (Nehemiah 8: 10) We become not just physically stronger, but our emotional and spiritual stamina increases as well.

So what about you? Are you being intentional and relational in cultivating your relationship with God first and then with others? If not, what do you need to change to make this happen?

May God grant us the joy of His presence so that we can be girded with His strength.

RELATIONSHIP

*"I will do for you all that you ask. All the fellow
townspeople know that you are a woman
of noble character." Ruth 3:11 (NIV)*

✝

My women's Bible group studied the life of Ruth for a series entitled *Critical Choices-Biblical Women Who Made Good Choices.* We also looked at the Proverbs 31 woman, who is often referred to as "a woman of excellence." Ruth, however, is the only historical Biblical woman who is actually described by name with that designation. The Greek word for "noble character" is "hayil;" it's the same Greek word that is translated *excellence.* Ruth made several key choices, including leaving her own country, culture, family, and religion to move with her mother-in-law, Naomi, to Bethlehem.

There are many lessons that we can learn from Ruth's life, including her commitment, devotion, and loyalty to her mother-in-law. Her famous words are often quoted at marriage ceremonies as words between a bride and a groom, but these are Ruth's words to Naomi when she was urged to return to her home in Moab:

> *"Don't urge me to leave you or to turn back from you.
> Where you go, I will go, and where you stay, I will stay. Your people
> will be my people and your God will be my God. Where you die, I
> will die and there I will be buried. May the Lord deal with me, be it
> ever so severely, if anything but death separates you and me."
> Ruth 1:16-17 (NIV)*

It's interesting to me that even though Ruth's legal tie with Naomi was severed by the death of her husband, the two women's friendship and commitment to each other remained in tact even to the point of living together! Their example continues to challenge me as a daughter-in law, and now, with Meredith's marriage, as a mother-in-law.

The book of Ruth is an inspiring love story that demonstrates God's providential care. Ruth wasn't looking for a husband when she found herself gleaning in Boaz's field, but she knew a good husband when she saw him! Following her choice to work in order to provide for her family, Ruth adheres to her mother-in-law's counsel and pursues a marriage relationship with Boaz. She actually asks Boaz to marry her! (Ruth3:9) Ruth knew what she was looking for and took a risk to get it!

Oh, that all of us, would follow Ruth's example and know, not just what to ask for, but what to become—a man or woman of excellence.

RELATIONSHIP

*"As the deer pants for streams of water, so my soul
pants for you, O God. My soul thirsts for God,
for the living God." Psalm 42:1-2 (NIV)*

Several years ago I stretched my comfort zone by joining the flower guild at my church. I had long admired the beautiful flower arrangements that appeared each week on the sanctuary altar. To be honest, I had no clue how the flowers got there—all I saw was the finished product. I wanted to learn the ins and outs, not just of flower arranging, but also the logistics—where to buy, what to buy, and how to design and select color schemes. In other words, the nuts and bolts, of what it takes from start to finish to produce such a work of beauty.

I openly admitted to the Flower Guild team that I knew nothing about flowers but was willing to learn. To their credit, the women patiently mentored, modeled and taught me the little I now know. I marveled at how well they used the resources that they already had—containers, supplies, last week's flowers lovingly preserved in the flower cooler. Step-by-step, through small group sessions, I learned about floral design.

One week I was paired up with an accomplished wedding floral designer who was not only more experienced, but who would also be out of town on the week of our flower guild duty. Her only instructions were to buy five hydrangeas at the wholesale florist, and put them in a basket. The thought of going and buying five any color, any size hydrangeas, and someone else picking up the tab made me giddy. I selected two blue, two pink, and one white—all big, beautiful, and blooming. I dropped off the flowers making sure I watered them before leaving.

The next day when I got to the flower room I discovered, to my horror, that the white hydrangea was as limp as a dishrag. Every bloom was shriveled and wimpy looking. "Water, it needs water!" I thought. I misted the blooms. Nothing happened. I watered the pot. No change. Finally in desperation, I took the whole pot and turned it upside down in the water bucket. Not even that helped—the hydrangea failed to "bounce" back. Another team member suggested doing an alternate design with the four remaining hydrangeas.

Sunday morning I arrived at church early to make sure the other flowers hadn't died as well. They still looked beautiful and healthy. Imagine my surprise, however, when I got to the flower work room and saw the white hydrangea blooming and robust—full of color and the picture of health. I was amazed at the transformation. Then it struck me. *This must be a small glimpse at what the resurrection felt like*. The initial sorrow, death, shattered dreams and disappointment—all surprisingly replaced with life, hope, and joy. This memory, my memorial stone, reminds me of the coming resurrection.

More than that, however, the white hydrangea signifies my need for *living* water—the water of the Holy Spirit. We need streams of living water in the midst of our daily deserts. We can have eternal life—salvation—and still be limp and seem lifeless— apart from the Holy Spirit's work in our lives. Maybe you are like the pink or blue hydrangeas and bloom with "normal" watering, but I want to be like the white hydrangea—thirsty and needy—getting drenched in the life-giving living water.

"With joy you will draw water from the wells of salvation."
Isaiah 12:3 (NIV)

RELATIONSHIP

"You have instructed many; You have strengthened feeble hands;
Your words have supported those who stumbled.... But
now trouble comes to you and you are discouraged;
It strikes you and you are dismayed."
Job. 4:3-5 (NIV)

I found this verse while cross-referencing another verse. The words caught me by surprise, but really "nailed" me. The previous two months had been challenging as I dealt with acute arthritis attacks and the residual treatment and side effects. Having to slow down frustrates and annoys me because I typically have one setting—full speed ahead!

As I read the words, I realized that God knew me better than I know myself. I had not acknowledged—much less confessed—the discouragement, impatience, frustration, and anger directed at God for not providing me with immediate relief and healing.

I suddenly recognized that God, through His Word and in His faithfulness, continues to meet me wherever I am. The lyrics to Casting Crowns' song, *Voice of Truth,* assures each of us that Jesus IS the Voice of Truth.

> "Out of all the voices calling out to me
> I will choose to listen and believe the Voice of Truth
> For Jesus, You are the Voice of Truth."[12]

Jesus—the same yesterday, today, and forever—still tells us the truth. He cannot lie. Sometimes it's words we long to hear like Jeremiah 31:3 "I have loved you with an everlasting love." At other times, His truth may be a word of correction.

May this be the commitment of our lives—to listen, believe, and be changed by Jesus, the Voice of Truth.

RELATIONSHIP

*"The Bereans were more noble-minded than those in Thessalonica,
for they received the word with great eagerness, examining the
Scriptures daily, to see whether these things were so."*
Acts 17:11 (NAS)

I want to be like the Bereans—noble-minded and open to new ideas. The gospel or good news about Jesus was new to them; yet they were willing to listen to Paul's message. Not only were they willing to listen, they were also willing to learn. From this passage, we see that the Bereans were receptive and eager hearers. They were willing to examine the Scriptures for themselves and not just take Paul's word on it. The Bereans were diligent in their study, investing their time on a daily basis to seek the truth.

This is what I desire for my life: that I would listen, learn, be receptive and teachable, eager and diligent in my study and pursuit of the truth of God's word. The purpose of God's word is to change us more and more to the image of Christ—to give us not only head knowledge, but also heart knowledge.

Every verse of Scripture can be examined using the following acronym:

S - Sin to confess
P - Promise to claim
E - Example to follow
C - Command to obey
S - Stumbling block to avoid

In our verse today, the Bereans are an example to follow. The next time you read your Bible, think of the eager, teachable, diligent Bereans. Put your "SPECS" on, dig a little deeper and ask God to help you apply His Word to your life.

RELATIONSHIP

"For the message of the cross is foolishness to those who are perishing,
but to us who are being saved, it is the power of God."
1 Corinthians 1:18 (NIV)

One of my favorite pieces of jewelry is a large pewter cross
that a friend gave me for my fiftieth birthday. When I wear it (which
is often), I am not only reminded of Jesus' love for me, but my
friend's love as well.

One afternoon last week, I went to the United Cerebral Palsy
(UCP) Adult sheltered workshop to pick up Brucie. In the main
dining room there were many "clients" gathered together waiting on
buses or rides. When my son first started attending UCP, I was very
uncomfortable talking to the other clients because so many of them
were nonverbal. There are probably 120-plus disabled adults there
each day, all with multiple challenges. James Bruce is one of the
younger disabled adults. Since his entry into the program, I have
become much more comfortable in acknowledging the other disabled
clients.

On this particular day, a wheelchair-bound, large African-
American man caught my eye. One of his eyes is always closed, but
the one that was open was looking straight at me. I smiled and said,
"Hello." He started pointing and at first, I couldn't figure out what
he was pointing to. After looking around, I finally pulled out my
silver cross necklace and said, "My cross?" He nodded excitedly and
gestured for me to come closer. As I did, he clumsily reached into his
t-shirt and pulled out a beautiful gold cross on a gold chain. His smile
broadened as he showed his cross to me. Who would have thought
we had common ground? As I continued to admire his cross, I
realized that a raw form of communication had just transpired.

Our crosses had formed a silent connection between us that
transcended gender, race, culture, socioeconomics, and intellect.
Perhaps that is why so many folks in our society today are trying
desperately to remove any visible reminder of the cross of Christ.
Jesus' cross connects us not only to Him, but also to each other.

This incident, coupled with James Bruce's recent question to
me, "Mama, do you know what the cross means?" has tugged at my
heart over the last several days. All of us should be able to clearly
articulate what the cross means to each of us: forgiveness, second
chances, new life, and sacrificial love so powerful that I am granted
life when I deserve death. From now on, whenever I wear my favorite
cross, I will remember this man's look of pure joy when we both
realized that we were siblings—connected by the cross of Christ.
That indeed is no less than the power of God.

RELATIONSHIP

"Love one another deeply from the heart"
1 Peter 1:22 (NIV)

There are a number of "one another" verses in the Bible. It's God's guide for telling us how to live with and treat each other. Among the "other" verses, we are told to honor, accept, instruct, serve, greet, encourage, admonish, comfort, consider, forgive, be kind to, pray for and love one another. In fact, the "love one another" command occurs 12 times in the New Testament.

Something that God puts so much emphasis on should command our attention. The question is not, "Should I love?" but, "How should I love?" The answer is fleshed out in the rest of the "one another" verses. Love is not a feeling but a choice in action. When we choose to honor, accept, encourage, comfort, forgive, be kind to and pray for someone else, then we are choosing to love. When we are patient and kind, we choose to love. When we don't brag and aren't easily angered, we choose love. Paul says that love always protects, trusts, hopes, perseveres, and never fails. (1 Corinthians 13:7) Peter says that love covers a multitude of sins. (1 Peter 4:8)

We should look for ways to demonstrate love in action toward one another. Recently, I received a note from a former student that touched me greatly. She herself is a busy mom with four children under ten, but she carved out the time to jot down some encouraging words for me on a card, and also enclosed Daniel's recent news article. It's definitely *a keeper* and a reminder that it's the little acts—the attention to detail—being faithful in the things that the world will never applaud that are important to God who sees it all.

RELATIONSHIP

"Love your neighbor as yourself."
Luke 10:27 (NIV)

Adrien and her family returned to their native Hungary yesterday. Saturday morning we met for one last breakfast conversation at the coffee shop. She talked for an hour as I intently listened, occasionally asking her a question or two. I marveled at just how far she'd come with her proficiency of our English language and her walk with God. I'm not exactly sure what prompted me to ask her to share with me the most important thing that she had learned since coming to America, but I did pose the question. Her response was both quick and challenging. Three things stood out in her mind and heart as her most treasured lessons:

The value of common prayer.
The importance of a smile.
The blessing of getting a "win-win" situation.

When pressed further, Adrien went on to explain each lesson. "Robert and I have never before known the value of common prayer, but when our class prays together, things happen." She was referring to our own weekly Sunday school class and the time we regularly allot for specific prayer needs. The collective verbal prayer requests are then summarized and sent to each class member to promote additional prayer for these causes throughout the week. The requests range from salvation for a loved one, to finding a job or a house. Together we had prayed for the publication of Adrien's husband's research, the right schoolteachers for her children, a job for Adrien, childcare for her boys, and a host of other requests.

"There's nothing magic about our prayers," I said. "God loves to hear them and answer in His own way. Jesus said when two or three are gathered in My name, I am with them."

Adrien went on to explain that the value of a smile should not be underestimated. She said, "In my country, we were raised under communism and it strips the soul. No one smiles. Here in the South, everyone smiles!"

The final life lesson Adrien learned from co-workers at the hospital where she worked. After securing a job as a pharmacy technician, she got off to a rocky start with her co-workers. Somewhere along the way, she learned that you don't have to win every battle to win the war. In most cases of conflict, we can usually find a way for both parties to win something; thus the "win-win" concept. Once implemented and applied, Adrien's worst enemy became her best friend at work.

Three lessons from three different sources: the value of common prayer from friends at church; the value of a smile from a culture known for hospitality; and the concept of "win-win" from caring co-workers who cared enough to teach one who was willing to learn. The blessing for me is that I continue to learn from Adrien as well. She has taught me much during our time together, and I am grateful for her friendship, transparency, and willingness to learn about God and life.

What about you? Who is YOUR neighbor? Do you know the value of common prayer, the power of a smile and the blessing of cultivating a "win/win" resolution?

By God's grace, may Adrien's insight and understanding encourage, challenge and motivate us today.

TRUST

*"Let us then approach the throne of grace with confidence
so that we may receive mercy and find grace to
help us in our time of need." Hebrews 4:16 (NIV)*

The proverbial "ox was in the ditch" one Thursday night at the Evans' house. I was teaching a ladies Bible study on Thursday nights and childcare for James Bruce wasn't a problem, until this particular night.

Bruce's Friday night game was switched to Thursday night. Unfortunately, my normal "go to" childcare folks all had other plans. I considered canceling the Bible study when the woman who was hosting the study suggested that I bring Brucie with me. He could watch a movie while we had our Bible study. Reluctantly I resorted to her suggestion.

The irony of the situation was not lost on me as I navigated my way to her home. I had to concede that God definitely had a sense of humor. I told myself, "I'm leading a women's retreat this weekend studying the Red Sea Rules, and focusing on Red Sea Rule #1: 'God knows where you are and He means for you to be there.'"[13] I realized that by changing all of "my" plans, God was giving me an opportunity to practice what I'm teaching.

Our study was on prayer and we had a good session. After the study, we always have a prayer time where we put our weekly requests on an index card and exchange them with another woman. This person would become your prayer partner for the next week. The hostess and Brucie rejoined us for the prayer time. Knowing that he loves music, one of the women asked James Bruce if he would sing a song. His face brightened as he sang "Amazing Grace." We all clapped and then they asked him to sing another song. James Bruce looked as if he couldn't decide which one to sing. All of the other ladies drew a blank, not wanting to suggest one that he didn't know. I'm not sure why, it was the only song that came to mind at that point, but I suggested the old hymn "What a Friend we have in Jesus." Immediately, he started singing:

> What a friend we have in Jesus
> All our sins and griefs to bear
> What a privilege to carry
> Everything to God in prayer.

When he got to the last line, the rest of us caught our breaths. James Bruce summarized in one stanza what we'd spent the last hour studying. It was a "holy ground" moment for all—one where God says, "I'm here with you." God used my disabled son's singing to remind me that He does know where I am and He means for me to be here—in the midst of changed childcare plans, baseball season, raising James Bruce, teaching Bible studies and speaking engagements.

TRUST

"Do as You have promised."
2 Samuel 7:25(NIV)

David's prayer to God was pretty simple, yet profound. He reminded God to do or accomplish that which He had promised to do. In order to pray that prayer, we should know what God promises.

I thought to myself, *What has God promised?* For starters, He has promised that He is the God of all comfort; that His grace is sufficient; that He knows the way I take; that He will never leave or forsake me; that underneath are His everlasting arms; that He is able to do more than I can think or imagine; and that He has gone to prepare a place for me. All of those promises help us to trust His character and heart, even when we can't trust our circumstances.

TRUST

"Trust in the name of the Lord and rely on God."
Isaiah 50:10(NIV)

For some unknown reason, my body was attacking itself. Like an army, the attackers invaded my joints making simple tasks, like getting into a car, going up or down steps, or getting a shower, nearly impossible. I urgently prayed for relief and healing. In my daily Advent readings in Isaiah, I kept finding verses that reminded me to trust in the Lord and rely on Him (Is. 50:10). I then cross-referenced Isaiah 10:20 (NIV), "Truly rely on the Lord." Another one was Isaiah 26:4, "Trust in the Lord forever." A pattern emerged from the verses and I knew that God was telling me to trust and rely on Him.

My doctor prescribed a Medrol dose pack and a small measure of relief came, at least enough to allow me to attend a wedding on Saturday. During the ceremony, the minister kept admonishing the young couple to trust in God, rely and depend on Him. There it was again—God's message to me—only in a marriage ceremony that was literally fleshed out before my eyes.

You see, the minister was the groom's elderly grandfather. The very words that he was speaking to the young couple, he himself was living before all of us. To perform the ceremony, he entered the sanctuary in his jazzy scooter wheelchair accompanied by his oxygen supply. He himself was depending on God, and the means God supplied, to enable him to do what God had called him to do. It was, and always will be, one of the most meaningful marriage services that I have ever witnessed.

I got God's message to trust and rely on Him—in the pain, the hurt, the fear, the uncertainty, and also in the celebration, the joy, the happiness—trust not in your circumstances, but in your God.

Once again, God met me where I was, just as He did with the shepherds, wise men, Simeon, Anna, Mary and Joseph 2000 years ago. He still speaks through His Word, through our circumstances, and through His people. May we be willing to listen, to hear, and obey for only in obedience is there great joy.

TRUST

*"Now may our God and Father himself clear the
way for us." 1 Thessalonians 3:11 (NIV)*

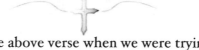

I discovered the above verse when we were trying so
desperately to secure James Bruce's critical UCP placement. He had
been on their waiting list for an adult workshop slot for ten years.
The only holdup was the state Mental Health Services allowing him
to accept the slot. We called, we pleaded, we reasoned, and we
prayed—all to no avail.

I found, claimed, and prayed this verse for James Bruce's UCP
placement. A little over one month later, the way had been cleared
for his placement.

When I pray, "clear the way," in my mind's eye, I see a
bulldozer knocking down mountains and filling up valleys in order to
clear our path. We have urgently claimed that prayer many times
since Brucie's UCP placement. We prayed it when Robert was
searching high and low for a car replacement. We prayed it when
seeking guidance in Daniel's college selection. We prayed it when a
mysterious ailment attacked my body leaving me with few answers
and relentless pain. When God doesn't answer as quickly as I'd like,
or in the manner that I anticipate, my impatience kicks in. I then
find myself weighted down with fearfulness, fretting, and anger.

One day when I was in my "fear and fret mode," I went to
Sunday morning service and our pastor's sermon was entitled, "The
Lord Will Provide." The sermon passage was from Genesis 22, where
God directed Abraham to sacrifice his son, Isaac. Three times, in this
one chapter, Abraham declares with confidence, "The Lord will
provide." I looked on my margin notes and I had written six prayer
requests, four of which had already been answered. The hymn
selection followed the same theme, and I found myself uplifted when
we began to sing the hymn, *God Will Make a Way*. All of a sudden, I
marveled at God's goodness in meeting me at a point of great need.
He promises to make a way for me, but in doing so, He expects me to
follow and to accept His leading.

Whatever the obstacle in your own life, pray that God Himself
will make a way and clear your path. Expect Him to act on your
behalf, and be sure to thank Him when He answers. When He clears
our way, He's not just changing our circumstances; He's allowing us
to know Him better.

"He who made a way through the sea and a path through mighty
waters...makes a way in the desert and streams in the wasteland."
(Isaiah 43:16-19 NIV)

TRUST

"Blessed is the man who trusts in the Lord whose confidence is in Him.
He will be like a tree planted by the water that sends out its roots by the stream.
It does not fear when the heat comes; its leaves are always green.
It has no worries in a year of drought and never fails to bear fruit."
Jeremiah 17:7-8 (NIV)

We'd just returned from a week at the beach where the seawater is very salty. The aftermath of the storm surge from Hurricane Katrina was evident, as much of the inland vegetation—trees, plants, and shrubs—didn't survive the damaging effects from exposure to the salt water. Thousands of trees were still standing, but they were dead with no leaves or fruit.

When we got back to Birmingham the first thing I noticed were the signs proclaiming, "Conserve Water-Level 2." I really didn't need a road sign to announce the very dry conditions.

As we drove through our state, we observed brown lawns and pastures, dry leaves, and scorched plants, not to mention a few dead trees. In fact, from our house to the highway, there were at least six large trees that had died.

The prophet Jeremiah was well aware of drought conditions. In the verses above, Jeremiah paints a vivid word picture of the contrast between a man who trusts in God and one who doesn't. Jeremiah knew that it was inevitable that heat would come, not "if" but "when." For the man who trusts in God and not in his circumstances, God's word promises that there will still be life and fruit—even in the midst of drought. The difference is the believer's root system. Jesus Himself promised, "Whoever believes in me,... streams of living water will flow from within him." (John 7:38 NIV)

Whatever we're going through, God knows where we are. If we're dry and need refreshment, He can and will renew us if we just ask Him. If we're like the tree planted by the water then we shouldn't fear or fret. We can be confident that God will be glorified as we bear much fruit.

TRUST

*"Let us fix our eyes on Jesus the author and perfecter
of our faith." Hebrews 12:2 (NIV)*

One afternoon while walking the high school track, I witnessed the high school band practicing under the watchful eye of the school's new band director. Listening to the Director's verbal commands to his students helped me to break the monotony of my exercise. Over-and-over again, the band marked time, marched with and without instruments, and counted. I went home from the track and could still hear the band director barking orders in my head:

"Maintain your intervals!"   "Unacceptable!"
"Keep your lines straight!"   "Stand up tall!"
"Point your toes as you march!"   "Snap to attention!"

My personal favorite was, "Don't look down where you're going—look up." At one point in last week's practicing, the band director had the band march down the field with their heads thrown back and their faces heavenward. There were audible groans as they first attempted this marching style; then peals of laughter erupted as they realized they could indeed march forward while looking upward. What is true for the band members is certainly true for us as Christians. So many times, we look down in discouragement and defeat, or we look around at our circumstances rather than looking *up* to Jesus. The writer of Hebrews encourages us to "fix" our eyes on Jesus. The Latin word for fix literally means, "to fasten into place." My eyes can't be fastened on my circumstances and Jesus at the same time.

Each day, probably hundreds of times daily, I have to decide where I will look and what I will see. Just as the band members needed encouragement, practice and discipline to find their focus, so do I. The more I discipline my emotions and practice looking up at Jesus, the more trained I become to do so.

So how about you? Are you looking down in discouragement at your circumstances, or up to Jesus? Today try marching down life's field while looking up to Jesus. It won't just change your scenery; it will also change your perspective.

"We live by faith, not by sight." 2 Cor. 5:7 (NIV)

TRUST

*"Trust in the Lord with all your heart and lean not on
your own understanding; in all your ways acknowledge
Him and He will make your paths straight."*
Proverbs 3:5-6 (NIV)

Bruce and I attended Daniel's graduation from Auburn University. We joined thousands of proud family members and friends to celebrate the students' achievement. Auburn's commencement speaker was Tim Cook, current CEO of Apple®, a 1982 Industrial engineering Auburn graduate. In his remarks to the students, Cook shared some personal discoveries from what he described as a most improbable journey.

Cook left Auburn in 1982 and headed for graduate work at Duke University. After receiving his MBA, Cook joined IBM® and Compaq®. In 1998, he was offered a position at Apple®. At that time, Apple® was a company on the verge of collapse. There was no iPhone®, iPad®, or even iPod®. Engineers are trained to analyze data and to evaluate both the costs and benefits of different options. Cook's engineering background made staying with Compaq® the logical and wisest career path.

Against family members' counsel, mentors' advice, and the overall probability of the cost/benefit analysis, Cook trusted his gut-instinct and made the career move to join Apple®. Cook considers this decision to be the single most important one of his career. Today Apple® is one of the most successful companies in the world. Cook's first piece of advice to the graduates was simply: "If you listen to it [intuition] it has the power to direct you or redirect you in a way that is best for you."[14]

Cook's second point was to make sure you prepare well. "Intuition should never be a substitute for planning and preparing. For all of us intuition is not a substitute for rigorous thinking and hard work." Cook quoted Abraham Lincoln who once said, "I will prepare and some day my chance will come." He also referenced the Auburn Creed, which in part states, "I believe in work, hard work."

Finally, Cook encouraged the new graduates to make sure to execute their plan. "Intuition is critical, but ultimately meaningless, if not followed by relentless preparation and execution," he explained. He then closed by saying, "Let your joy be in your journey."

I've thought a lot about Tim Cook's remarks. Surely, there's a lot to be learned from someone else's life experiences, but Cook's counsel is not God's counsel. Today's verse tells us to trust in the Lord, not in ourselves. In fact, we're specifically warned in Scripture about not trusting in our own understanding, but to instead acknowledge God in all of our ways and He will direct our paths. This is the difference between a Biblical world life view and a secular one. Cook's points regarding preparing, planning, working hard and executing are applicable for each of us, no matter where we are in our life's journey. The question each of us must answer is this: Will I trust God or will I trust myself?

Jesus said, "What good will it be for a man if he gains the whole world, yet forfeits his soul?" (Matt 16:26 NIV)

Choose life. Choose God. While there's nothing wrong with Abraham Lincoln's quote on preparing for our "chance," I much prefer Charles Kingsley's advice, "Have thy tools ready and God will find thee work."

TRUST

"Let go displeasure."
Psalm 37:8 (PBV)

✝

Meredith is in a women's small group Bible study that meets weekly at 6 a.m. The group's leader asked each woman to think of a word to describe their prayer priority focus for the year. Each woman had a week to reflect and pray for her personal focus word. The next week each of them wrote their word on a prayer card and shared why they chose the word.

The results were interesting to say the least. Two women chose "faith" or "by faith;" others chose peace, priority, organization, gratitude, and "much more" (as in much more grace, strength, and whatever else God chooses to give).

I've thought (and prayed) a lot about this exercise over the last two weeks. I tried several words to describe my own yearly priority focus, but none of them felt right. The words that kept coming back to me weren't the ones I wanted to hear. Finally, I was able to accept the two words as my yearly priority; *the doing*, however, will be much more difficult.

My two words are "let go." It's not just the "let go, and let God" thought, but rather the actual physical release of letting go of people, attitudes, and actions. I made a whole page of things to let go—starting with my four children. As a Mama, it's difficult to turn loose, but I need to practice it more.

The next big "let go" was fear. I made a lengthy list of things that I fear from James Bruce losing his spot at UCP to providing enough funds for his care after we're gone. I included everything from singleness for my adult children to where they might be if they marry or take jobs across the country. Every time I thought I was through, God kept saying "What else?" I kept writing until finally God said, "Okay, now let it go."

There are other things on my "let go" list: worry, doubt, anger, bitterness, and even "stuff" as in material possessions. I read a book this week entitled *Living with Less*[15] by Mark Tabb. His one point is that the only way to get more out of life is to choose less...less stuff, less activity, less wanting more. He encourages readers to simplify your lifestyle and deflate your opinion of yourself.

We can all make our own "let go" lists. The good news is that as I open my hands and heart to let go of fear, stuff, children, and expectations, then I am truly free to accept what God chooses to give—peace, faith, guidance, contentment, and purpose. I also have more room and ability to "Hold onto" those things that God says to hold onto—to Him, instruction, courage, and confidence.

So what about you? What would be on your personal "let go" list? What is your prayer/priority focus for this year and what will you change in order to make that happen?

"May He work in us that which is pleasing to Him."
Hebrews 13:21 (NIV)

TRUST

"I will give you treasures of darkness."
Isaiah 45:3 (NIV)

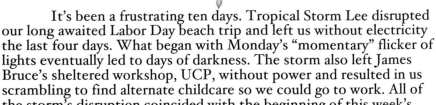

It's been a frustrating ten days. Tropical Storm Lee disrupted our long awaited Labor Day beach trip and left us without electricity the last four days. What began with Monday's "momentary" flicker of lights eventually led to days of darkness. The storm also left James Bruce's sheltered workshop, UCP, without power and resulted in us scrambling to find alternate childcare so we could go to work. All of the storm's disruption coincided with the beginning of this week's women's Bible study on 2 Timothy, "Lectures, Letters and Legacy."

Knowing that Satan loves to distract, disrupt, and discourage us whenever God is at work in our lives, I shouldn't have been surprised by the timing of my circumstances. A ruined beach trip, a soggy lake outing, no child care for James Bruce and four days with no morning coffee and regular quiet time, all added up to a complaining and grumbling spirit. I tried to "count it all joy" (James 1:2) and "in everything give thanks" (1 Thes.5:18), but I kept coming back to a self-imposed pity-party. After all, I was trying to finish the teaching preparations for Wednesday night's initial study and I needed power to do so.

Tuesday night, by candlelight, I prayed—well, more like demanded—"God, please help. I NEED electricity. The church needs electricity. What about the Bible study? You can do ALL things. I need power to finish my preparations."

All of a sudden, I felt God reminding me that I already HAVE power, and it's not electrical; it's the presence of God Himself. God IS with me—in light and in darkness. He's with me when the vacation days are perfectly cloudless and He's with me when they are washed out. Much like Paul, I experienced the reality and truth of 2 Corinthians 12:9 (NIV). "My grace is sufficient for you, for my power is made perfect in weakness."

Saint John of Avila once wrote, "One act of thanksgiving when things go wrong with us is worth a thousand thanks when things are agreeable to our inclinations." About the time I tried thanking God for the darkness, instead of demanding that He remove it, I heard James Bruce singing from his darkened room:

"Oh how I love Jesus
Oh how I love Jesus
Oh how I love Jesus
Because He first loved me."

With those words, light dawned in my heart and spirit. I remembered finding today's verse "I will give you treasures of darkness" in 1989. We had just completed five-year-old James Bruce's genetics studies when I realized that there could be—and indeed would be—some treasures of darkness, or valuable life lessons, given in our special needs journey. Our electricity wouldn't be restored for another 40 hours, but I started looking for other "treasures of darkness." Among them:

> Chick-fil-A® biscuits and hot coffee for breakfast.
> The husband who went and got them.
> Flashlights and candles that reminded me even a little light is a lot of help in total darkness.
> Cooler temperatures that made the September nights bearable without air conditioning.
> James Bruce's singing which reminded me that it's better to sing than "stew and brew."

There are other things on my treasures of darkness list, but you get the idea. I don't want to live in darkness, but I'm grateful for the perspective I've gained from the last ten days.

Wherever you are today, ask God to, not only show you, but also give you "treasures of darkness" which provides those lessons that can't be learned in the light and easy times of our lives.

MERCY

*"The Lord is close to the brokenhearted and
saves those who are crushed in spirit."*
Psalm 34:18 (NIV)

Hurricanes Dennis and Emily stirred up not only the ocean, but also the seashells. Bruce, James Bruce and I had a glorious time last week picking up shells along the beach at Gulf Shores.

Hundreds of shells lined the beach. At first, we just filled buckets as quickly as possible, but as the week went on and the abundance became overwhelming, we started getting really picky with our criteria; keeper-shells had to be large with no chips, holes, or rough edges. They had to be unusual in shape or color to be deemed worthy of being kept.

As our seashell hunting continued throughout the week, my thoughts turned to thankfulness. How glad I am that God is not a vacationing seashell hunter, with a list of criteria for what He keeps and what He discards. He not only keeps the broken hearted and crushed in spirit; He looks for us and seeks to find us. Jesus said in Luke 5:31-32, "It is not the healthy who need a doctor, but the sick. I have not come to call the righteous but sinners to repentance." Unlike our seashells, we don't have to be perfect to come to Jesus—we can be chipped, worn out, broken, and rough around the edges or even have a hole in our heart.

May we all experience and share the good news of Jesus—that He has come to bind up the brokenhearted, free the captives, and to comfort all who mourn.

"He bestows a crown of beauty instead of ashes, the oil of gladness instead of mourning, and a garment of praise instead of a spirit of despair, so that our lives are a display for His splendor." Isaiah 61:3 (NIV)

MERCY

"It is for freedom that Christ has set us free."
Galatians 5:1 (NIV)

Patrick Henry once said, "Give me liberty or give me death." To him and many of the other founding fathers, life and liberty were synonymous.

Indeed, the Greek word for freedom is "euletheria." It means freedom, liberty, autonomy, privilege, and independence. In classical Greek, euletheria was essentially the right and power of self-determination, the state in which one can act and move without restriction or hindrance. Biblical freedom is the believer's status before God in which he ultimately lives under divine authority and not human authority. He therefore submits to civil government and its laws as an accommodation for the sake of God's will. All of these concepts are found in the document we call the Declaration of Independence.

Twenty-seven of our 47 founding fathers had formal theological training. Modernists try to rewrite or reframe our nation's history to remove all references to God and His role in our nation's birth. It is clear, however, from the first words of the Declaration that the men who wrote it shared some fundamental values. Listen to the opening words of the Declaration:

> "We hold these truths to be self-evident, that all men are created equal, that they are endowed by their Creator with certain unalienable rights, which among these are Life, Liberty and the pursuit of Happiness..."

Our founders believed in absolute truth; they believed we are created (not evolved); they acknowledged a Creator; and they cherished life, freedom, equality, and the pursuit of happiness.

Likewise, Jesus as our Savior has set us free from the bondage of sin and death. In John 8:32 Jesus said, "You shall know the truth and the truth will make you free." (NKJV) Truth is not just the words in our Bibles; truth is a Person. Jesus, the Son of God, also said "I am the way, the truth and the life; no one comes to the Father but through Me." (John 14:6) Let us celebrate our nation's birth and independence, but let us also celebrate our dependence on God and His redeeming work through Jesus Christ.

MERCY

"Blessed are the merciful for they will be shown mercy." Matthew 5:7 (NIV)

My sister, Jan, was driving after dark the other night when she had a tire that was dangerously low. She stopped at a truck stop, but had trouble getting air into the tire. A driver for a local bottling company asked if she needed help and then proceeded to put air into her tire. When she thanked him, he simply responded that he hoped someone would do the same for his wife if she were ever faced with a similar situation.

As Jan was telling my mother the story, she went on to describe her earlier experience last week in a local doctor's office. She was completing some paperwork when an elderly gentleman started talking to the receptionist. His voice was low, but pleading, "Ma'am, I really need to see the doctor today. Can't you just bill me the co-pay?"

The receptionist was polite, but firm. "No sir. We can't see you today until you pay the co-pay from the last visit plus today's visit."

At that point, my sister returned her paperwork and asked if she could help. The receptionist told her how much the co-pay amounts were and Jan wrote a check to cover them.

"What do you want from me?" the old man asked incredulously.

"Nothing," Jan said, pausing briefly before adding, "except maybe a hug."

As the old man hugged her, he said, "Ma'am, are you an angel?"

This week is Easter week. The reality of Easter—Christ's crucifixion, death and resurrection—is that He paid a debt He didn't owe so that we didn't have to. Indeed, we had debt we "couldn't" pay. Jesus Christ, not an angel, but the very Son of God paid the entire debt—and not just the co-pay. Like the elderly man, we may be wondering in response, "What do you want from me?"

The answer is simple—first, believe and receive. "Yet to all who received Him, to those who believed in His name, He gave the right to become children of God."(John 1:12 NIV) Then after we receive His gift, He bids us, "Follow Me."(Matthew 9:9)

Jan was following Jesus when she paid the elderly man's co-pays and she received mercy when the truck driver helped her at the gas station. In God's economy, obedience always brings blessing.

GIVE THANKS

"One of them, when he saw he was healed, came back, praising God in a loud voice. He threw himself at Jesus' feet and thanked Him." Luke 17:15-16 (NIV)

On His way to Jerusalem one day, Jesus was met by ten leprous men who asked him to have pity on them. When he saw them, he told them to go and show themselves to the priests. As they were going, they were healed. One of them returned to fall at Jesus' feet and thank Him.

If the statistics from this gospel narrative are accurate, it explains why gratitude is such a rare commodity. Ten men were healed; only one took the time to say "Thank You."

Ellen Vaughn, in her book entitled *Radical Gratitude*, challenges each of us to "Be the one." She adds:

> "Cultivating a grateful heart is not just an add-on nicety as we steamroll through our day. A posture of purposeful, perpetual thanks to God is absolutely central to Christian character. It gives glory to Him. It is the key defense against Satan's temptations to despair, distrust, and dysfunction. It protects us from sin and self. It is the hallmark of heaven. It does not exist in hell."[16]

In our own family, Daniel, is the one who constantly demonstrates and challenges me to exhibit gratitude. This morning, after a bowl of cereal and a toasted bagel, he told his Dad, "Thanks, Dad, breakfast was good." I was thinking it was just a bowl of cereal and a bagel, but he is thankful anyhow. I was reminded that I, too should be the one to express gratitude for food, family, provision, and a husband who helps me.

Most of us could probably muster giving thanks for being healed or an answered prayer. Paul tells us to "give thanks always in all things" Ephesians 5:20. Whatever our situation or circumstance, may each of us "Be the one" to give thanks and praise to God.

GIVE THANKS

Autistic kids are typically sensory defensive. For most, this means an aversion to physical touch and an extreme sensitivity to noises. Factor in being mentally challenged and scared to death and it's easy to see how getting James Bruce's teeth cleaned presents a difficult endeavor.

Fortunately, there is a group of talented folks who are willing to take on the task. They cajole JB into laying down on a "table" and then six of them Velcro his wrists and ankles and then papoose him mummy-style. Brucie screams and cries, begging them to let him up, but they continue, ignoring his desperate pleas for help. They clean his teeth, x-ray, and finish the oral check-up. I, on the other hand, go out to a small courtyard to pray so that I don't have to listen to his anguish.

One day when I took James Bruce to the pediatric dentist, I was allowed back in to see him when the dental team finished. James Bruce was drenched with sweat—shirt, hair, and face. His cheeks were red and he'd been crying, but as he got up from the dental chair, he brushed his teeth with his finger and said, "Thank you for cweaning (cleaning) my teeth and thank you for my toothbrush!" There wasn't another sound in that room. All of us stood there in amazement. Finally, an older dentist looked at another team member and said quietly, "Guys, when one of these kids says 'thanks', this makes it all worth it. That's why we're here."

So many times in my own life, I kick and scream out not to God, but AT Him. Only later, (how I wish it would be sooner!) that I realize that it was out of His love for me that He didn't grant my prayers the way I wanted. His goal is to "clean me up" conforming me more and more to His image—making me more like Jesus. He is more concerned about my character than my circumstances.

Today, let's all "be the one" who quickly says and mean "Thank you," to God, our family, friends, and those who help us throughout the day.

GIVE THANKS

"This is the day the Lord has made;
we will rejoice and be glad in it."
Psalm 118:24 (NIV)

Wednesday afternoon after work, I picked James Bruce up from United Cerebral Palsy's (UCP) Adult Services Center. As he bounded into the car, James Bruce was smiling and I could tell he'd had a good day.

"How was your day?" I asked.

"Mama, Mama, I had a good day! How was your day, Mama?" he asked excitedly.

"Actually, my day was good too. What did you do at UCP today?"

"I made money!" he said emphatically. With this declared he turned to drinking his Arby's Jamocha shake (his daily reward for being good at UCP) and listening to his music. I silently prayed and thanked God again for UCP—not just the facility, but its wonderful staff and leadership. Five days a week, they give James Bruce the gift of place—not just a physical space, but a place where he's accepted, affirmed and allowed to grow. This literally allows me to work and to regroup for his daily care.

That night after dinner Bruce and I were sitting on the front porch, drinking coffee, and watching James Bruce roam through the front yard. I told Bruce that James Bruce had told me about his good day at work.

His daddy smiled and shouted to him, "Did you have a good day?"

"Yes," he replied.

Bruce followed up his response with another question. "What made your day so good?"

"God did!" Brucie quickly answered and then went about dropping more pine straw in the yard.

Bruce and I sat there and laughed—both stunned and quickened by his answer. The simplicity and directness, the confidence and assurance that God had indeed given him a good day caught both of us by surprise. Most of us say the right thing—that every day is a gift from God—but few of us embrace the concept as James Bruce did. I remembered that Jesus taught his disciples "the kingdom of heaven belongs to such as these." (Matthew 19:14 NIV)

Oh, that all of us would be as quick to give God the praise and glory for our good days and great blessings. God wants all of our lives to be a living testimony to the value of knowing Him.

PRAYER

"After they prayed, the place where they were meeting was shaken." Acts 4:31 (NIV)

✝

This is the kind of prayer I long for now. A powerful, impact prayer that makes a difference in the lives of people, and brings God glory. Most of the time, however, the display of impact prayer—the shaken meeting place—is absent. However, the impact of our prayers should never be underestimated. God still listens, hears, and acts whether I *feel* like He does or not. My prayer-power is not dependent on my feeling, but on His faithfulness.

I thought about this a lot the afternoon that I received the news that a dear friend's mother had died from an apparent heart attack. Overwhelmed, I started cooking potato salad and pound cake—comfort food for me at least. God gently reminded me of John Bunyan's classic quote, "You can do more than pray AFTER you have prayed, but you cannot do more than pray UNTIL you have prayed."

"Now to Him who is able to do exceeding abundantly beyond all that we ask or think." Ephesians 3:20 (NAS)

PRAYER

"Why are you sleeping? Get up and pray."
Luke 22:46 (NIV)

I stumbled across these words from Jesus as I looked at all of his references to prayer in preparation for a study that I taught. Jesus' words were the first words on my mind and heart as I woke one morning. There was no more sleep to be had. I knew this was not just an invitation, but also a command to pray.

Now I know that Jesus slept—like the rest of us. He was asleep in the back of a boat in the middle of a storm when the disciples were sure they were all going to drown (Imagine sleeping in a boat through Hurricane Katrina). He also prayed all night before he chose the twelve apostles (Luke 6:12); and in the morning while it was still dark (Mark 1:35), and at night on a mountaintop by Himself. If Jesus needed to pray, how much more do I?

"Whatever you ask in prayer, believe that you have received it, and it will be yours." Mark 11:24 (NIV) Ask...believe...receive. Prayer is a process of asking God to do what only He can do and being willing to accept His answer.

Charles Spurgeon once said, "Don't pray for the work (of ministry), prayer IS the work."[17]

PRAYER

"Why are you sleeping...get up and pray?" Luke 22:46 (NIV)

My latest sacred echo began with Laura Black's talk at church. Laura began her story by detailing a humorous story from her honeymoon 12 years ago. She and her husband, Bill, had booked a "semi-inclusive" resort. Instead of everything being paid for in full, they had credits from which to choose. One of the credits was for a continental breakfast. Bill and Laura are both breakfast lovers and so decided on the front-end to bypass the continental breakfast and splurge for room service. For $14 each, they both got an omelet, some fruit, a muffin and a small glass of orange juice. For six days, the hotel wait staff brought them their room service breakfast. Bill and Laura would go out to the lanai, eat breakfast, and talk about how marvelous it was.

On the last day in Bermuda, Bill and Laura decided to just go downstairs to the continental breakfast and skip their little private treat. Once there, Bill and Laura were astonished to see dining room tables set with white linen tablecloths. Soft jazz played in the background. The butter was even molded into little rosettes. There was a four-foot ice sculpture in the middle of an eight-foot round table laden with fruit. A hotel server manned a beef carving station. The continental breakfast turned out to be a rich feast. They had missed it for six days because they didn't get up and go.

Laura told the story to illustrate a spiritual principle. God's Word is good and sometimes we flip a calendar and read a verse on it or read a short devotional and get something special out of it. There's nothing wrong with this, but if that's ALL we do with God's Word, we're likely to be settling for a $14 omelet and missing the full feast. Laura says:

> *"There is so much more waiting for you. A table has been prepared just for you. But you have to get up. You've got to make the effort to walk to it. And when you do, you'll find the sweet music of Jesus playing in the background. Staples will have been formed into little rosettes just for you. There will be the choicest meat to truly sustain you. There are even things of beauty in the middle of the sweet nourishment, just for you. But you've got to get up. At some point we have GOT to STOP trying to squeeze a little bit of the gospel into our great big ole' lives and start PRAISING GOD for the privilege of being able to squeeze a little bit of ourselves into the great big old gospel. But you have to get up and then you've got to get down on your knees, then stand up and be prepared to be used mightily."*

At 5:30 a.m., it was cold and dark as my alarm went off. Every ounce of my being wanted to stay in that bed, roll over, and go back to sleep. Instead, I heard my sacred echo, "you gotta get up." Once my heart heard those four words, I was awake. I rolled out of the bed, grabbed a robe and headed to the kitchen for coffee. Some 75 minutes later, my heart (and my journal) was full from God's feast. Like Jeremiah, I could truly say, *"When your words came, I ate them; they were my joy and my heart's delight, for I bear Your name."* (Jeremiah 15:16 NIV).

So what about you? Are you dining each morning with a feast from God's word or are you settling for $14 room service? You gotta get up and go to the banquet prepared by God just for you.

PRAYER

*"But the angel said to them, 'Do not be afraid. I bring you good news
of great joy that will be for all the people. Unto you is born this day
in the city of David a Savior who is Christ the LORD.'"*
Luke 2:10-11 (PBV)

Each year as the Christmas season arrives again, I eagerly
anticipate the Christmas Advent season. In our family, we light the
Advent wreath candles every night and have a short devotion. The
ever-increasing light is a reminder that Jesus is the light of the world.
The candles are symbolic for various aspects of Christmas. We light
the first candle for *preparation*; the second one stands for *celebration*;
the third one represents *joy*, while the fourth one stands for
revelation. Another variation has the candles representing fulfilled
prophecy, Bethlehem, shepherds, and *angels.*

The Greek word for "angel" is "angelos," which means to
announce, bring news, or bear a message. It turns out that angels
were present at several different points of Jesus' life:

- His conception was announced to his mother Mary (Luke 1:26-28)
- His physical birth was announced to the shepherds (Luke 2:8-14)
- His resurrection was told to the women outside His tomb (Matthew 28:2-7)
- His ascension was witnessed by the believers (Acts 1:11)

Angels will continue to play a prominent role in the work and
life of Jesus. According to Matthew 16:27, "the Son of Man is going to
come in His Father's glory, with his angels, and then He will reward
each person according to what he has done." The angels who
announced Jesus' first arrival will accompany His second coming.
Only this time, Jesus won't be a babe in a manger, but He will come
as King of Kings and Lord of Lords.

As we look back to Bethlehem and remember Christ's birth,
we celebrate His life, atoning death, and resurrection, and look
forward with hope and anticipation to His second coming. The
celebration of the first Advent or arrival is a reminder that Jesus is
indeed coming again.

There are many ways to celebrate the season of Advent.
Regardless of which format you choose, remember to *prepare* your
heart to *celebrate* with *joy* the *revelation* of Jesus Christ.

PRAYER

Yesterday when I left work, I went to pick up James Bruce from the UCP workshop. As I left the hospital parking deck, I started praying about a situation that has caused me to "press hard into God." There are times when we pray, when we really do want the right answer, whatever it is—as long as it's the right one. Author Jan Karon, in her Mitford series, calls it the prayer that never fails—"thy will be done."[18]

When James Bruce got into the car, he started singing. If he's had a good day, he starts singing right away and wants me to sing with him. I wasn't in much of a singing mood, but his selection of song, quickly caught my attention:

> "O Lord, you have been good,
> you have been faithful to all generations...
> For by your hand we have been fed
> And by Your Spirit we have been led."[19]
> -Twila Paris

I quickly joined him with singing, reminded once again that God IS good... He IS faithful... He does feed and He does indeed lead... one generation to the next. I also remembered a quote from Phillips Brooks, "Prayer is not conquering God's reluctance, but taking hold of God's willingness."

PRAYER

*"When you pray, keep alert and be thankful.
Be sure to pray that God will make a way"
Colossians 4:2-3 (CEV)*

✝

I taught a women's Bible study focusing on Robert J. Morgan's wonderful little book, *The Red Sea Rules*. Using the Israelites' story, the miraculous crossing of the Red Sea, Morgan offers ten sound strategies for moving from fear to faith. *The Red Sea Rules* reveals, even in the midst of seemingly impossible situations, God promises to make a way for us.

During the study, I shouldn't have been surprised to find myself in seemingly impossible situations. Among them:

- A 34-year-old extended family member diagnosed with a brain tumor.
- A friend facing foreclosure and financial difficulties.
- A longed for adoption held up by international red tape.
- A single mom facing emotional and financial distress with her children.
- A friend bound in the cycle of addiction.
- A young couple lost their child.

The list went on and on...seemingly endless and, without God, virtually hopeless. The Christian, however, is never hopeless or helpless. So I prayed. "God remember (insert name). Please make a way. Do it in a way so that they get the victory and You get the glory."

To my knowledge, there was no immediate "parting of the Red Sea" in any of the dozens of situations included in my prayers. Still there was a peace and a sense of God's presence. When I opened the church bulletin on Sunday, one of that morning's selections was a song entitled, "God Will Make a Way." We just sang the chorus a couple of times, but I knew that God was meeting me where I was—and, in fact, doing it with a sense of humor.

As a prelude to our upcoming missions conference, I had been reading a book about Isobel Kuhn, a missionary with the China Inland Mission. She writes, "I have found that if we go as far as we can, God often opens up the rest of the way."

Whatever the impossible situation is in your own life, pray that God will make a way.

"Keep on praying." Ephesians 6:18 (NIV)

PRAYER

"Beginning to sink he cried out, 'Lord, save me'!"
Matthew 14:30 (KJV)

James Bruce hopped in the car one afternoon after a day of "work" at UCP's adult sheltered workshop. He was clutching a piece of paper as he excitedly said, "Mama, Mama! Here's my complication."

My heart rate cranked up a notch as my pulse began to race. Pieces of paper sent home usually mean a bad report for James Bruce's behavior. As I took the piece of paper from James Bruce's hand, I saw the title on the page. It read, "The art of conversation." Relieved, and almost giddy with a reprieve from a bad behavior report, I marveled that someone was intentionally taking the time to try to improve James Bruce's conversation skills.

For most of us, the idea of prayer is much like James Bruce's mix-up. Prayer tends to be more *complication*, than *conversation* with God.

Today's scripture passage is a familiar one. Jesus' disciples were out on the lake one night when they saw Jesus walking on water. Peter asked to join Him and Jesus agreed. Peter got out of the boat, but took his eyes off Jesus, looking around instead at the wind and the waves. When Peter lost his focus, he began to sink. Terrified, he cried out, "Lord, save me!"

Writing about this passage in his book, *Morning and Evening*, Charles Spurgeon makes the following points about prayer:

"Sinking times are praying times..."
"Short prayers are long enough."
"Our extremities are the Lord's opportunities."[20]

Peter started out of the boat without praying, but once in danger, cried out to Jesus. His prayer, though late, was not *too* late. There were but three words that Peter gasped out, but they were sufficient for his purpose. Not length, but *strength* is desirable. A sense of need is a great teacher of brevity.

One of the best ways that I've found to pray (and I'm still learning!) is to use Scripture and take it back to God. Some of my favorite verses include:

"Strengthen my hands."(Nehemiah 6:9)

"Do not let the hardship be insignificant before you." (Nehemiah 9:32 NAS)

"Oh God,... we don't know what to do, but our eyes are on You." (2 Chronicles 20:12 NIV)

"Bless these boys." (Genesis 48:16 NIV)

"Spread your protection over them." (Psalm 5:11 NIV)

"Bless all his skills, O Lord, and be pleased with the work of his hands." (Deuteronomy 33:11 NIV)

"Pray to the Lord your God that He would tell us where we should go and what we should do." (Jeremiah 42:3 NIV)

That's just a sample of some of my prayer verses that I've found helpful. The verses say in just a few words what the deepest desires of my heart are. Prayer in its simplest form is a conversation with God, but it's a two-way conversation. We don't just talk; we also listen. Two of the tips on James Bruce's conversation sheet included maintaining eye contact and listening to the other person. If we did that in our prayer time, our prayers would be much more conversational and much less complicated!

Every day is an opportunity to pray.

"Lord, teach us to pray." (Luke 11:1)

GROWTH

The American Humanist Association unveiled a provocative $40,000 holiday ad campaign for Christmas one year. The ads proclaimed, *"Why believe in a god? Just be good for goodness' sake,"* all over Washington, D.C. buses. In lifting lyrics from "Santa Claus is Coming to Town," the Washington-based group was wading into what has become a perennial debate over commercialism, religion in the public square, and the meaning of Christmas.

Part of me was shocked, indeed grieved, that a municipal transportation system would accept money to mock God, especially at Christmas as most of the world prepares to celebrate the birth of Christ. The other part of me wanted to shout, *How can one be good without God? Without God and His Word, the Bible, telling men what is right and what is wrong, who decides what is 'goodness' and once defined, how is it achieved?*

I eventually came to realize that the Washington ad campaign isn't anything that God hasn't seen before. Throughout history, men have worshipped false gods. From Baal in the Old Testament to the Greek's "unknown god" in the New Testament, and Buddha in the Far East, man has worshipped. As I reflected on the ad words, "Why believe in a god?" I realized that at least that part of the ad is correct. Why would anyone want to believe in just "a god?" What is the difference between "a god" and "*the* God?"

God knew that man, made in His own image, would worship something. This is probably the reason the First Commandment of the Ten Commandments is to have no other god before Him. That command includes ourselves. One commentator writes, "Perhaps the best definition of an idol is something we ourselves make into a god. It doesn't have to be a statue or a tree. It can be anything that stands between us and God or something that we substitute for God."

For the American Humanist Association, the substitute for God is self. However, this is nothing new. Back in Genesis 3:5, Eve was tempted by Satan to be "like God." The result was man's fall, sin, death, and separation from God. The good news of the Gospel, especially at Christmas, is that God still makes a way for His people to be reconciled to Him through the birth, life, death, and resurrection of Jesus Christ. As Christians, we need to be prepared to say, "We don't believe in *a* god, but we do believe in Jesus who proclaimed Himself to be, not *a* way, but *the* Way, *the* Truth, and *the* life."(John 14:6)

May each of us be prepared to proclaim, not just with our lips, but also with our lives, "Our LORD is greater than all gods." (Psalm 135:5 NIV)

GROWTH

"A woman who fears the LORD, she shall be praised."
Proverbs 31:30 (NAS)

My Bible study group did a series called *Critical Choice: Women Who Made Good Choices.* We looked at biblical women who made good critical choices and changed, not just their lives, but also the lives of those around them. Ruth chose marriage and Hannah chose children, but some of the women aren't as well known. There were five women who chose life for Moses and five daughters of a man named Zelophehad who chose boldness in prayer. In fact, their plea to Moses for a share in their father's inheritance actually is the first recorded women's rights case. The Daughters of Zelophehad's request wound up changing Israel's inheritance laws for all women.

We laid a framework for our study by examining the Proverbs 31 woman, often referred to as a "woman of excellence." Actually, we could probably refer to her as "the woman most women love to hate!" The Proverbs 31 woman is a nameless ideal who gets up early, stays up late, and never seems to rest. She works outside her home, yet never to the detriment of her family. Her husband and children rise to bless her, leaving the rest of us wondering, *how could I ever be this woman?*

To gain a proper perspective, we need to understand that this passage is not a day in the life of every woman, but rather a *lifetime* of good choices. The woman of excellence is both skillful and successful in her work and relationships. The key to her success is that she "fears the Lord." In other words, what she does is a byproduct of *who* she is, and what she is—a woman who fears the Lord.

Our take away or life application from this lesson was that a woman of excellence is a woman of influence. A woman of influence is one who displays *character, competence,* and *connection.* When character (who I am) is combined with competence (skillful ability) AND I connect with people (relationships) then I will be, by God's grace, a woman of influence. All three elements are essential for living a life of excellence and influence.

- Character - who you are when no one else is looking
- Competence - being good at doing what you do
- Connecting - to God and other people; cultivating relationships

So what about you? Do you connect to those around you at work, in your neighborhood or community? How about connecting to those in your family? Perhaps, you're connected to folks, but your work or habits are just average? Do you need to improve your productivity or the quality of your workmanship? Perhaps it's your character that needs some work. If so, now is a great time to re-evaluate what you read, what you see, how you talk, and how you spend your time and money. Often *good* choices are the enemy of the *best* choices.

"If you are going to achieve excellence in big things, you develop the habit in little matters. Excellence is not an exception, it is a prevailing attitude." Collin Powell

Character + Competence + Connection = Influence/Excellence

Make the BEST choice!

GROWTH

"Above all else, guard your heart."
Proverbs 4:23 (NIV)

"Watch over your heart with all diligence."
Proverbs 4:23 (NAS)

This is one of those great "life verses." Here the author of Proverbs warns us to guard, watch over, protect, and defend our heart diligently.

A few thoughts come to mind when I read this verse:

1. Guarding my heart is an active, not passive, process.
2. It is my personal responsibility—not someone else's.
3. It should be a top priority in my life.
4. It's a lifelong process. I will never arrive at the point where I don't have to guard my heart.
5. It's hard work—it doesn't just happen.

When Meredith, our oldest child, was born, I remember being overwhelmed with the weight of responsibility that I felt for her well-being. She slept in a cradle in our room for a few months. One night we moved her to her nursery crib. Although it seems silly now, I spent several hours on the floor of her nursery just to make sure I could hear her breathing.

Oh, that I would have the same diligence in protecting my own heart from what I see, what I hear, bad attitudes, and poor choices. Charles Spurgeon says, "No man ever fell into error through being too watchful."[21]

GROWTH

*"Stop thinking like children. In regard to evil
be infants, but in your thinking be adults."*
1 Corinthians 14:20 (NIV)

Almost every newspaper or magazine that I pick up these days has an article dealing with the growing obesity epidemic. It's not that people aren't eating—they're not eating the right food or getting the proper amount of exercise. In other words, they're not fit.

The same thing can be true for Christians. We're not feeding ourselves with God's word or exercising properly by applying His word to our lives. What should a FIT Christian look like?

The three characteristics of a FIT Christian—one that is healthy, growing, and exercising—are that he/she is:

- Faithful
- Intentional
- Teachable

One who is faithful is there for the long haul. One who is intentional lives life with purpose and deliberate action. The teachable person is the one who is willing to learn.

So how's your fitness in your Christian life? Are you growing, living life with purpose, willing to be stretched and taught, and then demonstrating faithfulness?

I am indebted to Dr. Harry Reeder, Senior Pastor of Briarwood Presbyterian, for his thoughtful insights, "Faithfulness is the banner of heaven. It's the welcome sign that says 'Well done, thou good and faithful servant.'"

GROWTH

"You'll never be what you're not becoming... dig deeper."[22]
-Paige Benton Brown

That was my one gold nugget from the 2006 PCA women's conference in Atlanta. Whenever I attend a retreat, seminar, sermon, or conference, I always ask God to give me a gold nugget. What is a gold nugget? It's a spiritual truth that gives you hope or help in daily living—a sort of modern day proverb or practical application that is often easy to remember, but hard to obey.

Some gold nuggets are such treasures that they have become part of the fabric of my life. These include:

- "Discipline your emotions."
- "Do your next thing."
- "God always answers prayer to demonstrate either His sufficiency or His supremacy."
- "Choose faith, not fear."
- "Decisions have consequences."

Since that particular retreat, I continued to ask myself, "What am I becoming?" That question has driven me to ask, "What do I want to become and how do I get there?" The first part of the question has an easy answer—I want to be more like Jesus. The second question—the "how to?"—is much harder.

In her talk, "What We Really Need to Know," Paige Brown shared the story of a family living in a New York City apartment. New Yorkers don't have yards—they have "outside space." This family wanted to renovate their apartment's outside space and make it safe for their small children. They consulted a fence company who promptly installed a three-foot fence around the "outside space." The kids were contained, but all the digging aroused a rat infestation. The company decided to go deeper with the fence—first six-feet, then nine-feet, twelve-feet, and finally fifteen-feet-deep. This is how far they had to dig down in order to secure the area. She used that story to challenge us to dig deeper into Christ, with His Word, prayer, forgiveness and power.

Much of my Christian life is spent dealing with the same old issues—fear, anger, impatience, bitterness, pride, insecurity—those "rats" that rob me of peace, joy and strength. It is only as I dig deeper into Christ and continue to turn those areas over to Him, that I, by His grace, can secure those areas and become more like Him.

So what about you? What are YOU becoming, and how are YOU going to get there?

May each one of us become and be called, "oaks of righteousness, a planting of the Lord for the display of His splendor." Isaiah 61:3 (NIV)

GROWTH

*"For the word of God is living and active
and sharper than any two edged sword."*
Hebrews 4:12 (NAS)

There are seasons of waiting in all of our lives—those times where we have to remain inactive or stay in one spot until something anticipated occurs.

A particular season of waiting for my family occurred near the end of my Daddy's life. My Dad remained in ICU in critical, but stable condition—on a ventilator and dialysis for two weeks. Two weeks seemed like two months as the stress and waiting took an emotional toll on all of us.

One Sunday, as I was praying, I impatiently told God—*healing or heaven*. Later I cross-referenced a verse (Isaiah 5:19 NIV) that nailed me:

> "Woe to those who say, 'Let God hurry, let him hasten his work so we may see it.'"

Those words are a vivid reminder that God knows where we are. He knows me better than I know myself. Whether it's waiting to see how baseball works out for Robert, or mates for my children, or post-high school plans for James Bruce, or even waiting to see what happens with my Daddy—God is in the waiting too. In light of eternity, two weeks is not even a speck on the radar screen.

GROWTH

"Enlarge the place of your tent...spread out."
Isaiah 54:2,3 (NIV)

God sometimes chooses ordinary objects to teach extraordinary life lessons. Jesus, the greatest Teacher who ever lived, used loaves and fishes, light, mustard seed, lost coins and sheep for illustrations of the truths He shared. Lately, in my own life, God has used pansies to keep giving me object lessons.

At Thanksgiving, I bought several pots of pansies. I meant to plant them, but never got around to doing so. Obviously, the pansies didn't grow very well because there was no room for them to grow. They couldn't spread out in the pots and became root bound. When the heat came, they wilted quickly.

Daniel, my youngest child, was quickly approaching high school graduation. I knew that he had good roots, but I also recognized that he needed room to grow. I started missing him even before he left for college. Yet, just as my pansies needed room to grow in order to reach their full potential, Daniel also needed some space. He has never known life apart from helping care for Brucie. He needs to learn life skills as well as engineering, his major. He needs to catch a vision of a world outside our home.

When we enlarge the places of our tents, our sphere of influence also increases. Jesus commanded the disciples to go into the world and preach the gospel, yet until persecution came, most of them remained fearfully huddled in Jerusalem. As they were scattered across the world, their influence, as well as the gospel message, went out into the world.

My prayer for each one of the young people who are graduating, getting married, entering the work force or military service, is that God will enlarge the places of their tents. As they go, may they take Him with them, spreading the good news that Jesus died so that we can live, both now and forever.

"Oh that You would bless me indeed, and enlarge my border, and that Your hand would be with me." 1 Chronicles 4:10 (the prayer of Jabez)

GROWTH

"To one who knows the right thing to do and does not do it,
to him it is sin." James 4:17 (NAS)

One morning while driving James Bruce to UCP, I heard a radio sermon by Alistair Begg entitled, "God of the Ordinary."[23] Alistair did a series of sermons on the book of Ruth. In this day's sermon, Alistair noted that Boaz was committed to doing the right thing. He said that each of us should ask ourselves every day, "What is the right thing to do?"

My office is about three blocks from the parking deck so I had a little bit of time to reflect on what I had just heard. As I walked into the hospital lobby, the headline of USA Today's newspaper (January 30, 2007) grabbed my attention. It read, "It was the right thing to do."[24] I was stunned. The same phrase that I had just heard on the radio was on the front page of USA Today. God, the God of the ordinary, was extraordinarily getting my attention.

The quote was from one of the co-owners of Barbaro. The 2006 Kentucky Derby champion horse had broken his leg in the Preakness and against all odds waged a courageous one-month recovery. The whole country had followed his progress and setbacks. In the end, however, the horse was euthanized the day before the article ran. When asked about reaching the decision to euthanize the horse, one co-owner wisely observed, "Grief is the price you pay for love." The other co-owner simply responded, "It was the right thing to do."

Barbaro's owners didn't take a poll to gauge public opinion; didn't worry about a public outcry; didn't consider all the financial gain that would be lost from breeding the horse. They just recognized the right thing to do and did it. Like Boaz, they risked personal loss, in order to do the right thing.

Whatever decisions we face today, let's start by asking the question, "What is the right thing to do?" Then when we know the right thing, let's be quick to do it.

GROWTH

*"Let no debt remain outstanding, except the continuing
debt to love one another." Romans 13:8 (NIV)*

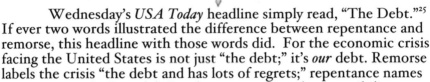

Wednesday's *USA Today* headline simply read, "The Debt."[25] If ever two words illustrated the difference between repentance and remorse, this headline with those words did. For the economic crisis facing the United States is not just "the debt;" it's *our* debt. Remorse labels the crisis "the debt and has lots of regrets;" repentance names it, appropriately, "our debt" and accepts personal responsibility.

Two weeks ago in Washington, DC, my youngest son, Daniel, and I stood at the top of the Washington Monument and looked out at the sprawling city. Our tour guide informed us that monument construction stopped in the 1840's because the government ran out of money. The work resumed in the 1870's and was completed a few years later. No funding, the Civil War, and national reconstruction all contributed to the 30-year delay. I was looking out one observatory window when Daniel quietly asked me, "Mom, do you get it?"

Puzzled, I responded, "Get what?"

"They stopped building because they didn't have the money; we would have borrowed and kept building," he said.

God's Word is very clear; debt is bondage. As I again looked at the *USA Today* headline, a little chorus from, Ellis J. Crum's song in the 70's came to my mind:

> He paid a debt He did not owe
> I owed a debt I could not pay...
> Christ Jesus paid a debt
> That I could never pay.

As you read and listen to all of the news surrounding our debt crisis, take a few moments and thank God for the One who removed the debt of our sin by shedding His own blood on the cross. Christ Jesus, who "gave His life as a ransom for many." (Matt 20:28 NIV)

GROWTH

"But you, keep your head in all situations."
2 Timothy 4:5 (NIV)

I've enjoyed walking at the nearby school track this week. The weather has been great, and football practice has been intense. You can tell that coaches and players have stepped it up a notch on emotion and preparation. Playoff hopes are on the line tonight. It's as simple as win and continue to play or lose and stay home. Preparation, attention to detail, focus and hard work are evident.

The Apostle Paul didn't coach a football team; he was a life-coach who mentored men. His favorite student was a young man named Timothy. Paul's last letter to Timothy, written just before Paul's death, is 2 Timothy. In chapter four, Paul reminds Timothy of the most important principles to remember. These are the things Paul wanted Timothy to recall when Paul is no longer there to remind him. The list could be a football coach's list. It includes the following:

Remember the game plan (God's Word)- 2 Tim 4:2
Be prepared – 2 Tim 4:2
Practice and get it right verse 2
Work hard – verse 5
Persevere and be faithful – verse 5
Do your best – verse 9, 21
Keep your head in all situations – verse 5

Paul ends his letter to Timothy by reminding him that Paul is about to die. He knows he has fought and finished well. This is my prayer for the team tonight and indeed their lives. May they fight and finish well for His glory. God never calls us to be successful, but He always calls us to be faithful.

GROWTH

*"This is to my Father's glory, that you bear much fruit,
showing yourselves to be my disciples."*
John 15:8 (NIV)

✝

Every day for the last three weeks, I've felt like Julie Andrews in *The Sound of Music* when she sings, "These are a few of my favorite things."

Our yard is full of flowers—eight different kinds of roses, fragrant gardenias, and lots of hydrangeas. The roses are red, yellow, pink and salmon-colored and have exotic names such as "Velvet Fragrance," "Remember Me" and "Touch of Class." The gardenias are beautiful in their white simplicity, but literally breathtaking with their fragrance. Then there are the hydrangeas, my favorites—white oak leaf hydrangeas, blue and pink Endless Summer hydrangeas, and blue Nikko hydrangeas. Even some hybrid pink and green hydrangeas have rooted on their own. To top it off, the cut flowers are filling almost every vase and container that I have. When the first rose bloomed, I gently cut it and placed it in one of my favorite Waterford vases. I don't have that many fine vases, but I have two special friends who've made sure that I at least have some Waterford crystal vases. When I start filling them with cut flowers from my yard, the vases remind me of my friends' generosity. The flowers also remind me of Bruce's vision to plant with a bountiful harvest in mind.

Our journey with hydrangeas began several years ago. At a time when we had kids in college and our money was really tight, I asked for "a" hydrangea for my Mother's Day gift. Bruce went and bought eight plants and I almost had a heart attack! Of course, nothing bloomed that first year. A couple of the plants had to be moved the next year when we realized they weren't getting enough sunlight. Eventually, however, the hydrangeas grew and bore beautiful blooms. Now each year as they bear fruit, they continue to bring me endless pleasure. They also take me down memory lane to that first Mother's Day when I looked at them and wondered if they would ever bear blooms on their own.

Without a doubt, my flowers bring me much joy as I admire their blooms, colors, and fragrances. It's not the leaves that bring me pleasure—it's the fruit. As Bruce and I cut blooms and fill vases, I'm already scouting out more buds to replace the flowers that I've just cut. I'm always looking for more blooms.

The other day I thought about today's verse—"this is to my Father's glory that you bear much fruit"—and wondered, "Am I bearing fruit? If so, how much fruit am I bearing? Does my fruit bring Jesus joy?"

Jesus went on to command his disciples to bear fruit—fruit that will last. We do this when we obey His commands, walk in the Spirit, and produce the fruit of the Spirit: love, joy, peace, patience, kindness, goodness, faithfulness, gentleness and self-control. (Galatians 5:22-23) Unlike *my* flowers, this kind of fruit WILL last, not just this growing season, but also through eternity.

So what about you? Are you bearing fruit for God's glory? If so, what kind of fruit are you bearing and what can you do to be more fruitful? Jesus' words to the disciples are still true today, "Apart from Me, you can do nothing" (John 15:5 NIV). God's goal for our lives is not just that we bear fruit or even that we bear much fruit. God's goal for our lives is that we bring Him much glory. John Piper says it well when he reminds us, "God is most glorified by me when I am most satisfied with Him."[26]

Oh that we would all live lives of fruitfulness and faithfulness and bring Him much glory!

GROWTH

"Strengthen my hands."
Nehemiah 6:9 (NIV)

✝

With all the images of the devastation from the Gulf Coast brought on by Hurricane Katrina, I still haven't been able to get the book of Nehemiah from my mind and heart. It isn't just the devastation, it's also the criticism, finger pointing, 20/20 hindsight, and blame gaming that is so wearisome.

Nehemiah faced the same sort of adversity. He had opposition from those who didn't want the rebuilding to move forward (does that sound familiar?), from those who were mistreating the poor by inflating prices and making large profits (chapter five), those who plotted and tried to stir up trouble (chapter four), and workers who were worn out and overwhelmed with the task of clearing the rubble in order to rebuild (Neh. 4:10).

Nehemiah faced his enemies, but he refused to *focus* on them. Instead, he devoted himself to work on the wall. (Nehemiah 5:16) He prayed, posted guards and prayed some more. He disciplined his emotions and did the next thing—whatever it was: guarding, building, carrying rubble or encouraging the people. By refusing to engage in defending himself, he didn't waste valuable time, energy or resources from carrying out his mission.

When the wall was successfully rebuilt in 52 days, even Israel's enemies "realized that this work had been done with the help of our God." (Neh. 6:16) In other words, the Israelites got the wall for protection, but God got the glory.

Let's pray that God will raise up godly Nehemiah-like men and women for rebuilding not only the Gulf coast, but also people's lives. We need leaders and workers with integrity, vision, focus, and hard work who are willing to ask God to strengthen their hands and hearts for the job at hand. May God strengthen our hands for whatever tasks He has entrusted to us whether it's raising children, taking care of aging parents, teaching a Sunday School class, being a good student or helping to lighten someone else's load by giving our resources or time.

"God's people have always, when in the worst of conditions, found out the best of their God."-Charles Spurgeon

REFERENCES

1 The Hiding Place. Dir. James F. Collier. Perf. Julie Harris, Jeannette Clift and Arthur O'Connell. World Wide Productions, 1975. Film

2 Buechner Frederick, "Message in the Stars." In *Secrets in the Dark: a Life in Sermons,* 18-19. San Fransisco: Harper Collins Publishers, 2006.

3 Foster, Richard J. *Celebration of Discipline: The Path to Spiritual Growth.* San Francisco: Harper One, 1998.

4 NORDEMAN, NICOLE. Lyrics. "Gratitude". *Woven & Spun,.* Sparrow Records, 2002.

5 White Dies Sunday Morning. Last modified Jan 6, 2005. espn.go.com/classic/obit/s/2004/1226/1953400.html.

6 Tim Keller. *The Upside Down Kingdom.* Sermon. Redeemer Presbyterian Church. Mar 21, 1999. http://sermons2. redeemer.com/sermons/upside-down-kingdom.

7 Maxwell, John."Encouragement: Paul Knew How to Boast About his People". In *The Maxwell Leadership Bible.* Thomas Nelson:, 202. p. 1469.2011

8 Harvey, Alec. "Selma's Kathryn Tucker Windham finds a storied life among Southern Ghosts." *The Birmingham News.* Oct 17, 2010.

9 Elliot, Elisabeth. "Defining Suffering". Gateway to Joy. Back to the Bible. The Good News Broadcasting Association, Inc. http://www.backtothebible.org/index.php/ Gateway-to-Joy/Defining-Suffering.html.

10 Platt, David. *Radical: Taking Back Your Faith from the American Dream.* Sister, Oregon: Multnomah Books. May 4. 2010

11 NEWSONG. Lyrics. "Before the Day". *Rescue.* Sony Music.2005. Audio CD.

12 CASTING CROWNS. Lyrics "Voice of Truth". *Voice of Truth,* Beach Street Records, 2003, audio CD

13 Morgan, Robert J. *Red Sea Rules: 10 God Given Strategies for Difficult Times*. Thomas Nelson. November 6, 2001

14 Cook, Tim. "Auburn Graduation Ceremony." Lecture. Auburn University, Auburn, AL, May 4, 2010

15 Tabb, Mark. *Living with Less: The Upside of Downsizing Your Life*. B&H Books, 2006.

16 Vaughn, Ellen. Radical Gratitude:Discovering Joy Through Everyday Thankfulness. Grand Rapids, MI: Zondervan, 2005

17 Spurgeon, Charles. "January 4th Entry." In *Morning and Evening: A New Edition of the Classic Devotional Based on the holy Bible, English Standard Version,* Revised and Edited by Alister Begg. Crossway Books. 2003.

18 Karon, Jan. *Out of Canaan*, New York: Penguin Putnam, Inc. 1997.

19 Paris, Twila. "You Have Been Good." *For Every Heart* Album. Star Sing Music. 1988.

20 Spurgeon, Charles. January 14. Morning and Evening

21 Spurgeon, Charles. March 14. Morning and Evening.

22 Brown, Paige Benton. "What We Really Need to Know," Presbyterian Church in America Women's Conference. Atlanta, GA. 2006.

23 Begg, Alister. "God of the Ordinary." From Truth for Life. Sermon. June 5, 2012.

NC 2701224 USA Today. "It Was the Right Thing to Do". 2007. Jan 30.

25 USA Today. "The Debt". 2011. July 27.

26 Piper, John. *Desiring God*. Sister, Oregon: Multnomah Publishers, Inc, 2003.